"Shelly Pierson's *Into Your Soul* paints with precision the picture of how and why our soul evolves from life to life. Profound client examples that illuminate our soul's journey and provoke your own thoughts open insightful personal windows. Wisdom and commitment to the work of Past Life Soul Regression are evidence that Ms. Pierson is a master with her craft. 'Realistic Life' through normal, expected hills and valleys are described as they elevate our soul's learning."

— **Dr. Linda Backman, Psychologist and Regression Therapist**
April, 2022
www.RavenHeartCenter.com
Bringing Your Soul to Light
The Evolving Soul
Souls on Earth

Into
Your
Soul

A BEGINNER'S GUIDE TO

PAST LIFE REGRESSION

SHELLY PIERSON, MBA

www.N2Souls.com

Edited by Barbara Kohl

Cover and interior design by The Book Cover Whisperer: OpenBookDesign.biz

979-8-9859909-0-4 Paperback
979-8-9859909-1-1 eBook

FIRST EDITION

DEDICATION

I DEDICATE THIS BOOK to the many beautiful souls who have supported me every step of the way in my regression work and publishing this book:

My husband, Glenn, for introducing me to new thought spirituality and for supporting my career change and adventure into past life regression therapy. He's been my number one supporter throughout my training, research, client work, and drafting this book.

My family and friends for their continued support and spreading the word about my profession and introducing clients to me.

My many clients who graciously agreed to let me include their stories in this book. Their challenging, heartfelt, and beautiful experiences are the reason I do this work. Without their stories, there would be no book.

The many clients who work with me—I have learned something new with each one of you!

I wish to add a special thank you to Scotty's family for allowing me to use his story. Scotty's life on Earth was way too short for what his family and I would have preferred, but we have learned it is not up to us to choose another soul's path. Scotty is a beautiful, gifted soul who has given messages to many of us since his passing. We know he is still with us but in a different form.

I extend heartful gratitude
and blessings to all of you!

DISCLAIMER:

I wish to clearly state that past life regression work should never take the place of medical attention. Throughout this book I share stories of clients who have found relief from emotional, physical, and mental challenges after a regression session, but only subsequent to unsuccessful medical treatments and consultations. Each client was familiar with past life regression work and had a "feeling" a session might be helpful.

CONTENTS

"You, too, can begin to release the habitual drama that seems to follow you and begin to create positive change on your journey."

CHAPTER 1

Introduction to Past Life Regression

I am writing this book for the beginner—those who have never heard of past life regression work and those who are new to it and want to learn more. Twelve years ago I had never heard of this topic, yet here I am, a certified past-life and between-life regression therapist who recently changed careers after thirty-plus years in the information technology (IT) industry. There is a reason you chose this book!

Many people ask me how on earth did I move from IT to past life regression work. It's an interesting story and one that will resonate with many of you who feel a calling to do something different, going outside your comfort zone of familiarity and security. For the rest of you, I hope this book opens your mind to other possibilities for gaining awareness and clarity, and bringing forth healing in your lives.

This book is also for those who are interested in or new to exploring reincarnation, past life regressions, and spirituality. I didn't learn about spirituality until I was in my forties. Apparently, I had other work to do before it was time for me to venture onto this path, a path that has been both typical and atypical. Some of you will resonate with my journey. My hope is that my story may start you on your own journey or, at least, confirm that the thoughts in your head are not silly.

I do this work because of the healing it provides to my clients. It is a service to others that I am honored to facilitate. While working in the business world and transitioning to my next career, I was surprised at the number of people who had never heard of past life regression work. More surprising were the number of interested people who responded with, "Tell me more about that." Now, during my speaking engagements and workshops, I am often reminded of how new or peculiar this topic is for many people—hence the writing of this beginner-level book.

As with any practice or study, many of us become

learned or knowledgeable in a topic and our understanding of the vernacular grows with experience. It's often easy to forget that not everyone understands the terminology. Therefore, my intent with this book is to begin at the basic level and build from there. My intended audience encompasses all persons who are open to the possibilities about life, past lives, the afterlife, and everything in between. It doesn't matter to me if you are religious, non-religious, spiritual, or agnostic. Your belief system is your own and I honor that. If you have an open mind and want to learn about past life regression, this book is for you. Again, there is a reason you chose this book.

Throughout the book I reference many accounts from my client sessions. I have consent from each of them to share their stories; to maintain their privacy I have changed names and other personal identification information about them.

Chapters 1 through 6 describe the specifics of how a past life regression works and why people choose to have a session. The tone may be reminiscent of academic textbooks since it's presented in a teaching or didactic manner. In Chapters 7 through 14, the tone softens as I elaborate on various aspects of *YOUR* soul that are brought to your awareness using past life regression. As a bonus, I have included my workshop exercises at the end of seven chapters (3, 7, 8, 9, 10, 11, and 12) to help you work through the concepts presented.

There are many terms in this book that may be new to you. Please reference the Glossary of Terms in the Appendix to review a list of these words and their definitions.

CHAPTER 2

How I Got Started

Most people who know I spent thirty-plus years working in the IT industry look at me and ask, "How did you get from there to doing *this*?" By "this" they mean becoming a past-life regression therapist with speaking engagements and a long list of clients. After decades of working in the IT field as a computer programmer, system designer, systems analyst, project manager, high-level administrative manager, and a short stint in academia as an industry professor, how *did* I get here?

To answer that question, I often state that I have observed three "tracks" in which people begin their spiritual journey:

People born with special gifts. These individuals go on to develop their gift to the point where they can help others. This is the case with many psychics, mediums, and shamans. Typically, such people recognize their gift early on, seek a mentor to help them hone their skills, and then proceed to use the gift to help others.

✿

People who have a near-death experience (NDE). Many people who survive a brush with death come back with a new awareness, clarity, insight, or a gift they wish to share with others. Some die during surgery or in an accident; when their heart stopped beating, they returned to life via medical intervention or they naturally came back on their own. Often such people return with newfound experiences, awareness of spirituality, increased knowledge, and helpful information to share with others. Many have written books about their NDE, describing what they saw, heard, and experienced on "the other side," and some have received beautiful messages to share.

✿

People who experience a traumatic event. These people experience a trauma, usually a major loss as in losing a loved one to death, a relationship ends or drastically changes, a job/career ends, or a very serious health diagnosis is received. These events are known to take many people into "the dark night of the soul," to a place where they are finally broken open, where they surrender and stop challenging everything. That is what occurred with the death of my youngest brother, Jimmy. His suicide broke my heart and took me to a place of surrender—I was transformed. This traumatic event knocked down the walls of my well-planned life and finally opened me up to many experiences that I would have ignored before his death.

Personal Story

I learned of Jimmy's death in July 2009 via phone call—he was thirty years old. Anyone who has experienced the sudden death of a loved one knows the shock and numbness that takes over your body upon hearing such awful news. Suicide, a last resort for people who have lost all hope that life will ever improve for them, is discussed further in Chapter 11. I will not use these pages to discuss the details of Jimmy's death, but rather explain how this traumatic experience triggered a series of interesting events that changed my life.

Not long after my brother's death, I could sense his presence around me. I do not have psychic or mediumship abilities; therefore, I could not actually view him or hear his messages, but I definitely felt the energy of his presence. In my own way, I began asking Jimmy questions in my mind such as, "Where are you?", "What do you do all day?", "Do you visit your children?" Two weeks later an acquaintance handed me a book and said, "I thought you might like to read this." It was titled, *Letters From the Afterlife* by Elsa Barker.

As I read the book, I realized I was getting answers to the questions I was asking my deceased brother. It occurred to me that perhaps this was his way of communicating with me. Two months later, I attended a talk presented by a local physician, Dr. Jeffrey D. Millman. He discussed his belief in reincarnation, his experiences with past life regressions, and specifically how meditation and such regressions helped him in his current life. He also mentioned several books that changed his life: *Many Lives, Many Masters* by Dr. Brian Weiss, *Journey of Souls* by Michael Newton, PhD, and *The Tibetan Book of the Dead*. I quickly purchased and read those books and soon found my interest in past life regression growing as more books, speakers, and workshops continued to attract my attention. I then veered onto a new career path! I say "new career path" because I spent over three decades working in IT and then suddenly my career took a 180-degree turn when I switched to past-life regression therapy.

Going from the corporate high-tech world to spiritual work is hardly typical but the gist of my story is this: I stopped over-thinking the opportunities being presented to me, as in "I'm too busy to read that book," "I don't have time to attend a weekend seminar," "I shouldn't spend money on that training," and so on; instead, I began walking through doors of opportunity that presented themselves. I bought and read the books, attended the seminars, listened to guest speakers, and proceeded into past life regression training. (See the Recommended Readings section in Appendix.) Doing this work helps individuals perceive obstructions in their life, remove blocks, and move on to the beautiful life they were meant to have. That is why I love doing this work.

Past-life regression work has been around for a long time but it did not become an established and accepted practice until the 1980s and 1990s when two well-trained and educated practitioners started writing books about the subject. Brian Weiss and Michael Newton have written a plethora of books, several of which are listed in the Appendix. I consider some of their books to be "the classics" due to their ground-breaking, deep dives into the realities of the work. A list of contemporary authors is also provided in the Appendix. There are many others who wrote about the phenomenon of past lives and past life regression (e.g., Jane Roberts) before the 1980s, but Newton and Weiss are the two I am familiar with.

CHAPTER 3

Signs That You Have Had Past Lives

"These are the signs you have been with the same souls in past lives. Whether positive or negative, our souls retain the memory."

As I meet people on my path, many open up to me about their thoughts of past lives when they learn about the work I do as a past-life regression therapist. These thoughts range from, "I don't know if I have had a past life," to "I think I died on the Titanic in a past life," to many others between these two notions. Following are a few signs you have had a past life or lives.

Visiting someplace new: Have you ever visited a place you've never been before and yet it felt familiar and comfortable, or felt like home?

Maybe you encountered the opposite feeling when you visited another place and immediately felt repulsed and just had to get away. I have heard stories from people who have traveled to a place new to them yet inherently knew that if they turned into a particular street, they would end up at a place that felt very familiar.

❦

A time in history: Are you attracted to certain time periods such as the Victorian era or any other specific era? Maybe you are extremely drawn to visiting lighthouses, WWII ships, or ghost towns in the West. Do you collect things specific to an era or incident such as Civil War paraphernalia? Are you drawn to Native American or other indigenous peoples' artifacts in general or specific ones, such as pottery or baskets?

❦

Fears and phobias: Is there something you fear or do you have a strong phobia that you cannot explain? Some common fears are deep or rushing water, confining or close places, darkness, choking, heights, and having something close to your neck. If in your current life, when you were very young and a mean kid held your head underwater and you almost drowned, that could definitely explain your fear of water. But if no similar incidents ever happened to you, then how can you explain such a fear?

Somatic issues: These are physical symptoms that are unrelated to any identifiable medical cause. While somatic symptoms can be symptoms of psychological factors in a person's current life, there are also many somatic symptoms that do not have a clear origin or cause.

One client had frequent pain on one side of his ribs but had no explanation of its cause. Upon visiting a past life, he learned that he had been stabbed in the same area and died of the wound. Our soul memory often brings unresolved injuries, pain, trauma, and issues from past lives forward into our current life.

Dreams: Can you vividly remember certain dreams, even years or decades later? Did the dream entail traveling with a group of people you do not know or visiting a place that didn't seem to be of this world? Did the dream take you to a place in today's world but at a different time in history?

❦

Fascinating people: Have you met someone in your life you immediately felt connected or close to even though you just met him or her? We often use the term "soul mate" to describe such people: a best friend, partner, spouse, or child. The same fascination can apply to someone we meet, but immediately feel repulsed by and cannot get away from them fast enough!

These are signs you have been with these souls in past lives. Whether positive or negative, our souls retain the memory.

All of the above are signs of experiences in a past life. Following is an interesting story of a client who came to see me in search of an explanation of a recurrent dream.

Personal Story

Gemma wanted to learn more about dreams she had since age two of being on the Titanic. At the time of our session, Gemma was in her early thirties. She easily relaxed and entered a past life scene. I asked her to describe what she saw and was experiencing in as much detail as she could.

First scene: "I am a man, aged twenty-five, wearing black, smooth leather shoes that lace with a cord type of shoelace. I am also wearing a business suit with a vest and button-down shirt; the suit fabric is a cotton/silk blend. My hair is slicked back and I am clean shaven. I am outside on the deck of a ship, looking out, observing the endless miles of ocean; I feel a breeze and I am in awe at how serene it is. I am alone at this spot on the ship and I am now looking at the sky and the nice sunset. It's cool outside but not too terribly cold. I am on this ship for a business trip, my boss made me go."

Next scene: "I am still on the ship and people are screaming. I hear a loud metal noise, I also hear classical music playing. I feel like I'm going to die, I am very scared, actually frozen in fear as I stand on the deck watching the people panic around me. There are too many people, it's too crowded to do anything, I feel stuck and now I feel water covering my feet, it's freezing. I look down and notice I am wearing a long wool business coat that was stylish for that time. I am starting to panic, I know I am going to drown and I am scared it's going to hurt. I miss my family at home (parents and siblings). Now the water is up to my hips, it's just a matter of time to let go. Now it's getting quiet, the water is up to my neck, it's extremely cold, paralyzing. People are now splashing and crying around me. I see a lifeboat in the distance. I feel scared and wonder why I cannot get to a boat. I am now completely submerged, it's so cold, I feel like falling asleep. Now I am just under the surface. I start to feel serene and at peace, there is nothing I can do but accept this, I am falling more and more into darkness. I don't feel cold anymore."

Exercise

The intention of this exercise is to help you recall any evidence that may suggest memories of your past lives. Listed below are six categories discussed in this chapter. Review each category and write down items that might have a tie to a past life for you.

- ✿ Visiting a new place that felt familiar
- ✿ Attraction to a time in history
- ✿ Fears and phobias
- ✿ Somatic issues
- ✿ Recurrent dreams
- ✿ People in your life who you have had an instant connection with, positive or negative

NOTES:

_____

_____

_____

_____

_____

_____

_____

_____

_____

_____

_____

_____

_____

_____

CHAPTER 4

Establishing the Foundation

*"Our soul guides are always, and forever, with us.
Even if there were times in your life when you felt
alone, your soul guide was there."*

I am often invited to speak to groups about past life regression. I like to begin my presentations with twelve foundational concepts to set the stage for the discussion. I have come to believe the following concepts derived from my training and research, and all are continually reinforced during each client session I facilitate.

Twelve Foundational Concepts

1. We are eternal souls having
   a human experience.

2. Our souls are on a quest to evolve.

3. Having human experiences
   enables our souls to evolve.

4. Each of us has a soul guide
   who is always with us.

5. Our souls choose a specific lesson
   to work on in each lifetime.

6. Our souls only select lessons that
   we are capable of taking on.

7. Our souls script the opportunities
   and challenges into each lifetime to
   help us work on our chosen lesson.

8. As humans we have "free will," which
   allows us to choose whether we will (or
   will not) work on our chosen lesson.

9. If we do not complete a lesson
   in a given lifetime, we get a "do-
   over" in another lifetime.

10. Do-overs are never punishment or retribution for not completing a lesson, they are simply another opportunity to work on the lesson.

11. As our souls evolve, the lessons become more difficult.

12. Once our souls have completed all of our lessons on Earth, we are no longer obligated to incarnate on Earth.

Expanding on the Twelve

We are eternal souls having a human experience. Our souls were brought into existence from the same loving source of creation that brought life to everything, and our souls will continue to live on into eternity. Many of us, including me, come from fundamentalist religious backgrounds. Many of these religions teach that the soul is eternal, yet many reject the belief in reincarnation.

Since I have always had a very logical mind, this did not make sense to me. I ask, if we are eternal souls and have only one chance at life on Earth, then how can we explain the vast variations in lives among people? For example, some people are born sickly while others are born healthy, some have prosperous lives and others live in poverty, some live long lives yet others die as young children. The list is quite extensive when describing the variations of human lives on Earth, but again, if your soul gets only one chance at a lifetime on Earth, where is the explanation for the variations and absence of fairness? What I mean by "absence of fairness" is this—why can't *ALL* souls have healthy, prosperous, and loving lives on Earth?

Questions like these were answered when I learned about reincarnation. Reincarnation made logical sense to me. Although some religions do not support reincarnation, there are many religious and spiritual belief communities that do.

Our souls are on a quest to evolve. After a soul is created, its journey to grow, develop, and learn begins. The new soul inherently *WANTS* to grow and evolve just as a baby naturally wants to develop by rolling over, sitting up, and crawling. A wonderful book that explains soul creation is *Journey of Souls* by Michael Newton.

Having human experiences enables our souls to evolve. The reason for this is that we learn lessons in the Earth dimension—oftentimes called "Earth school"—that we cannot learn in the soul realm. As I read Dr. Newton's books several years ago and realized that our souls learn much while in the soul realm, I did wonder at the time why our souls do not learn all we need to in that realm and bypass the Earth experience.

After much more reading and learning about the soul realm, I realized that the soul realm cannot teach our souls everything because certain conditions that enable learning do not exist there. The soul realm is a loving, compassionate, all-accepting dimension full of the loving light that is the grounding, the home, of our souls. For this reason, there are no conditions in the soul realm to teach a soul the lesson of forgiveness, for example, because there is nothing there to forgive.

The same goes for the lesson of compassion because the soul realm is a completely compassionate place. The lesson of loving ourselves cannot be taught there because in the soul realm we have complete love for *all*, including ourselves. Love is the core of our soul's existence; therefore, our souls must have incarnations on Earth to learn lessons not taught in the soul realm in order to continue to evolve. Our souls need to learn the many lessons that the Earth school has to offer.

꧁

Each of us has a soul guide who is always with us. When our souls are created, we are assigned a soul guide, an advanced soul who has completed all their Earth lessons; therefore, they are highly skilled in guiding and advising our souls on our respective paths. We are also assigned to a soul group made up mostly of new souls similar to ourselves.

The soul guide is charged with the care and guidance of the souls in the soul group. In your current life, while growing up, you may have come to know this special soul guide entity as a guardian angel. You may have referred to this guide as God, angel, or protector.

Our soul guides are always, and forever, with us. Even if there were times in your life when you felt alone, your soul guide was there.

I have had some clients who felt their soul guide was not with them at times when they really needed them in their life, only to hear from their guide during a regression that they *WERE* there but the client blocked them. There are times in our lives when we humans choose to not listen to the continual guidance from our loving guides, but our guides *ARE* nevertheless always present.

※

Our souls choose a specific lesson to work on in each life-time. Each time we come into a human incarnation, we choose a specific lesson to work on during that lifetime. We work with our loving soul guide before we incarnate to help us determine the next lesson we are ready to take on, and the recommendation is based on the lessons we have already worked on and completed in the past.

Examples of lessons include learning to love ourselves, to love others, forgiveness, compassion for others, humility, responsibility, patience, and tolerance.

※

Our souls only select lessons that we are capable of taking on. We never take on an Earth lesson that our soul is not ready for or equipped to handle. Before each incarnation we work with our soul guide to review the lessons our soul has completed thus far, and then *together* we decide which lesson our soul is ready to work on next. Some lessons are more difficult or considered to be more advanced; these would not be assigned to beginner-level souls. A simple analogy is math: we would not consider putting a third-grade student in a trigonometry class because the typical third-grader would not have the necessary skills to perform well at that level of math. If the third-grader progresses in the usual math-learning path, they would be ready for trigonometry in high school. Our soul guides help our souls choose the right level of lesson that we are prepared to take on.

Our souls script the challenges and opportunities into each lifetime to help us work on our chosen lesson. For each lifetime we script the main events, participants, challenges, and opportunities for that life before we incarnate. Although it may be difficult to consider challenges analogous to opportunities, in the soul realm our souls really do consider challenges to be perfect opportunities for our souls to work on a given lesson.

For example, if my soul (with guidance from my soul guide) chooses learning to love myself as my next life lesson, then I am going to need opportunities in that lifetime to help me work on that lesson. Those opportunities might come in the form of being born with a physical disability, having a verbally abusive and denigrating mother, or even choosing to have a physically abusive father, among many other scenarios. If you choose overcoming abandonment as your lesson, then you will need some forms of abandonment in your upcoming incarnation to help you work on that lesson.

❦

As humans we have the attribute of free will. As we come into this Earth dimension with an intended lesson and anticipated challenges, we also come in with the human attribute of free will that allows us to *decide* if and when we want to work on the lesson throughout our life. We also have free will to listen (or not) to the guidance from our soul guide.

Since our soul guide is always providing guidance for us, you might recognize the guidance as that *gut feeling* you get at times. We have free will to decide whether we wish to follow the guidance. If you picture your birth, life, and death as a straight line from one point to another, just know we never stay precisely on that straight line through the course of our lives. We weave on and off that line, our path, as we have free will to work on our lesson or not to do so. When we veer off our intended path, our guides provide us with many opportunities to steer us back towards our path; whether to take such opportunities is also a free-will decision. Suicide, in most cases, is a free-will choice.

❀

If we don't complete a lesson in a given lifetime, we get what I call a "do-over" in another life. We get to do it all over again. Although the lesson will be the same, the circumstances, characters, and situations will be different. If your soul guide and your soul, upon completion of a lifetime, decide that maybe your soul needs to work on some other lesson to better prepare you for the one you did not complete, then that is a perfectly viable scenario.

For example, maybe you chose standing up for yourself as your intended lesson but instead of taking on the requirements to complete that lesson you allowed yourself to be a victim of your circumstances. Perhaps your next lifetime needs to be one of learning to be independent in order to better prepare your soul for standing up for yourself in a future lifetime.

❀

"Do-overs" are never punishment or retribution for not completing a lesson. Do-overs are merely another opportunity. It's your soul and your soul guide acknowledging the following: "That was a tough lesson—here is what I did right and here is what I need a little

help with. Let's work on some things and then I will be ready to do it again." When you do it again, the situations may be a little different, the players may change, but the lesson is still the same. It's common that lessons have to be repeated, especially as they become more difficult.

As an analogy, imagine that your eight-year-old daughter is in the middle of her first day of equestrian English-riding lessons.

After she receives some coaching and training from her instructor, she gets up on the horse, goes around the arena, and then she falls off. The coach will not punish her for falling off the horse; instead, the coach will check to see whether she is okay, dust her off, give her some additional coaching to improve her skills, help her understand why she fell off, get her back up on the horse, and let her try it again. This is similar to what our guides do for us—a do-over is never punishment.

❧

As our souls evolve, the lessons become more difficult. The lessons become more difficult because our souls are ready to take them on. Again, it can take several lifetimes to learn a particular lesson. During one of my speaking engagements, a member of the audience asked, "I thought as we evolve our lessons would become easier. Is this true?" It's the opposite.

I like to use the American school system example of kindergarten through twelfth-grade (K-12) analogy: we would not teach first graders geometry because they are unlikely to be ready for it before high school. We teach the basics in the first few years of school and work our way up to the more difficult experiences. And if you devoted one lifetime for each thing you learned in kindergarten, then you would have to go through kindergarten several times to learn all the topics—colors, counting, the alphabet, and so on.

We typically do not see beginner souls engaged in difficult lessons like forgiveness or overcoming abandonment. Similar to the eight-year-old taking equestrian lessons, as she progresses through training over the years, her jumps become higher and higher, and more and more challenging.

Once our souls have completed all Earth lessons, we no longer feel the necessity to incarnate on Earth. At that point we basically graduate from Earth school and our souls move on to do work elsewhere. Some souls become soul guides, others may become teachers in the soul realm, and some become healers and lightworkers. There is a vast amount of work being done in the soul realm, and I do not attempt to cover those areas in this book.

NOTES:

_____

_____

_____

_____

_____

_____

_____

_____

_____

_____

_____

_____

_____

_____

_____

CHAPTER 5

Purpose of a Past Life Regression

Definition

A past life regression consists of the ability to visit a past life to learn how it is affecting your life today. Oftentimes our soul memory brings things forward from past lives to our current lives and these show up in our current lives as distant memories; physical issues; dreams; emotional blocks; or feelings of fear, remorse, sadness, loss, and more. Typically, a past life regression therapist will guide their client to a past life using a relatively light level (alpha) of hypnosis. Several scenes from that past life will be visited and the circumstances of that life are reviewed with the client.

My process for doing this work is the same as just mentioned—using a light level of hypnosis with my clients, which enables them with the ability to access memories of past lives. The information about all of our past lives is accessible to us in hypnotized states (see Chapter 6 for more detail on hypnosis). I facilitate the session; my client has the complete experience of visiting the scenes, experiencing the feelings, and getting an understanding of that past life. I like to clarify this up front because some people have experienced alternative methods of getting past life details, such as having a session with a psychic who has the ability to tap into past life details for the client. In this scenario, the psychic tells the client of the past life details. This is a wonderful alternative for people who find hypnosis challenging.

Personal Story

An example of how a past life can affect your life today is a client named Kimo, who had a fear of the dark. When he visited a past life scene associated with this fear, he saw himself as a male prisoner in a cell in a dark, cold dungeon with his hands tied behind his back. He got stabbed in the back and died in that dungeon. Kimo's soul memory carried fear of darkness from that past life to his current life. It's interesting to note that Kimo was also born with a birthmark on his back in the same spot he was stabbed in the previous life.

Another example is Scotty and his story is associated with a somatic issue: neck pain that could not be explained. Scotty was in his early twenties and had experienced neck pain most of his life, but he could not recall any accident, injury, or ailment that could explain the pain. His neck pain was becoming worse and would oftentimes cause painful migraines. During Scotty's regression experience, he visited a past life where he was a male soldier making rounds of different checkpoints in a vehicle with his partner who was driving. At one checkpoint Scotty saw himself get out of the vehicle and then a woman got in the passenger seat where he had been sitting. The woman's young daughter climbed into the back seat and Scotty got in next to her. Before Scotty's partner could drive away, a man stepped in front of the vehicle and pointed a gun directly at the woman. Scotty leaned over to protect the young girl in the backseat next to him. As the driver attempted to drive away, the man shot the gun, missing the woman but hitting Scotty in the neck. Scotty said he could feel his head pushed back against the seat when the bullet hit him and then everything went black. Scotty, as the soldier in that past life, died from that gunshot. As Scotty came out of his hypnotized state, he understood the source of his current life neck pain and migraines.

I spoke with Scotty five days after the session and he said he had not had any neck pain since his regression. Our paths crossed again several months later and then again a year and a half later—no more neck pain nor migraines. By seeing the source of his pain, Scotty was able to release it. This is a wonderful example of how visiting the source of an issue—in this case a somatic issue (neck pain)—provided the ability to clear the issue and leave it in the past.

Scotty did ask me at one point why his neck pain became worse around his twenty-second birthday. I explained that he probably reached the age in his current life that he had achieved in that past life when he was shot and killed. It is with a sad heart to report Scotty passed away a few years later. Scotty started as a client of mine and then became a friend. I share the heartbreak of his absence with his family and friends.

When we visit a past life, we go to the *source* of

an issue. The typical benefit of visiting the source is releasing the effects of the trauma, thereby releasing the carry-over into the present life. I have noticed with many of my clients that if they had a fast, abrupt, or violent death in a past life that their human form did not have a chance to come to terms with before death, then the soul can bring residual effects forward such as the fear of darkness or neck pain in the examples above.

An alternate example is Carl, a client who *was* able to accept a tragic death in a past life and not carry any residual trauma into his current life. Carl visited a past life where he was born in England to a wealthy family. As a young man he enlisted in the military to fight during WWII; he felt that it was his duty to serve and thereby was trained as a combat pilot. When his plane was hit by enemy fire, he was conscious as the wreckage plummeted toward the ground. He recalled his thoughts in those moments and he had no hard feelings about his impending death. He was proud to have served and he knew full well the nature of the risks of fighting in the war. At the end of his session, I asked Carl if he had any fear of flying in airplanes, and he said, "No." This is an example of a soul who had time to come to terms with a tragic death and did not carry residual effects of that death into a future lifetime.

Purpose of a Regression Session

In the business world, we often used the term "root cause analysis," which means that when dealing with an issue, go to the root cause and deal with it there. Most often, this is where the best solution will be identified and implemented.

Consider an example of dealing with a medical issue. If you suddenly had a strange rash on your skin and visited a doctor, that doctor may prescribe an ointment for you to rub on the rash to make it go away. In many cases, this works to eliminate the rash. But what if the ointment causes the rash to get worse and you return to the doctor, only to be prescribed a stronger ointment, possibly one containing a steroid? Now there is a risk of the side effects caused by the steroid.

Returning to the original doctor visit in this example, what if the intent of the doctor had been to see what *caused* the rash in the first place? In that case, the doctor would have asked basic questions such as: "Did you change laundry detergents?" "Did you eat something recently that you normally don't eat?" "Did you wear new clothing before washing it?" A doctor who asks such questions is trying to get to the root cause of the rash in order to deal with its source instead of only resolving the symptoms.

Past life regression work is similar to root cause analysis with regard to going to the source of the issue. If you go to a past life where you visit the source of your fear of darkness, then part of my job as a regression therapist is to help you see the source, understand there is no benefit in bringing it forward to the current life, and then release it. In most cases, this strategy works.

Healing

Healing is the principal benefit of past life regressions, and this is the reason I love doing the work. Many clients have come to me seeking information into why certain challenges are in their life such as recurrent patterns with painful relationships, sudden or chronic health issues, fears, and anxieties, all of which block them from living happy, fulfilled lives. I have conducted many workshops with the title, "Visit the Past to Heal the Present." There is something powerful about learning the cause of an issue that then allows us to move toward healing. All of us come into our current life with gifts to help others but many of us cannot access those gifts because we are dealing with blocks that hinder us. Some examples of *blocks* are distrusting people, feeling unworthy, not allowing people to love us, and inability to forgive. But when we become aware of and release the blocks, then we can open up and share the gifts that we came into the current incarnation to accomplish. We will venture more into this topic when I talk about types of souls in Chapter 8.

Curiosity

Some clients are just curious about their past lives and schedule a session to see what comes up. I will share the story of Lucien who wanted a past life regression with me because he was *curious*. He was twenty-one years old when he had his regression. During his session, Lucien visited a past life in which he was a gentleman about age forty and he was nervous during the first scene he visited. I asked him why he was nervous and he replied, "My younger wife is in labor with our first child." As we progressed through that scene, Lucien became emotional as tears started rolling down his cheeks. I asked him why he was upset and he told me his wife and baby died during childbirth. We proceeded with the regression, going through several more scenes in that past life, and we learned he never emotionally recovered from the loss of his wife and child; instead, he became a recluse and shut himself off from society. At the end of the session when Lucien was no longer hypnotized and we were processing the contents of the regression, he realized that the past life experience was the cause of his blocking love in his current life: because he was afraid of losing love again. He probably would have never realized why he blocked love without seeing the source of the block in that past life. After the regression portion of the session, Lucien admitted to me he never dated anyone for more than a month and now he knew why. When I talked with Lucien a year later, he told me he *intentionally* worked at his relationships since he no longer wanted to block love. People who are curious about past lives can learn something very valuable about themselves.

Unresolved karma

Here I describe how aspects of past lives can be brought forward to our current lives as unresolved karma. When our soul worked on a lesson during a past life, there may be unpleasant parts of that

lesson our soul brought forward to our current life
that appear as challenging feelings. To determine
whether this has occurred with a client, I ask their
soul guide whether my client brought any unresolved
karma from the past life into their current life. If
the answer is "Yes," then I ask two more questions:

- ✿ "What is the unresolved karma
  my client brought forward?"

- ✿ "What can my client specifically
  do to resolve that karma?"

Following are a few examples.

⋙ Leilani's soul brought *loneliness*
forward to her current life.

Shelly: What can Leilani do
to resolve that karma?

Guide: Connect deeper with people,
don't be so afraid to share your truth.

⋙ Rowan's soul brought *anger* forward.

Shelly: What can Rowan work
on to resolve that karma?

Guide: Forgiveness.

Shelly: What specifically can Rowan do to work on forgiveness?

Guide: Trust other people.

⋙ Seanté's soul brought *resentment* forward.

Shelly: What can Seanté do in her current life to resolve the karma?

Guide: Acceptance of life circumstances.

⋙ Kaia's soul brought quite a bit of unresolved karma to her current life but she mainly needs to work on calmness.

Shelly: What can Kaia do to work on calmness?

Guide: Meditate.

Personal Story

Next is another example of a client who was curious. Mateo wanted a regression because he was curious about what a session might bring forth, and he also mentioned having obsessive-compulsive disorder (OCD) regarding excessive handwashing and locking doors. The session begins, and Mateo visits a lifetime as a marshal in the old West. In the beginning scene he is alone, riding his horse in the mountains; he is sad and angry.

Mateo then recalls a preceding event in that past life where he had arrived home to his small ranch and found his wife and young daughter murdered and all of their livestock stolen.

In the next few scenes, he tracks the band of murderers and thieves through a couple of states and ends up in Texas. He has killed some of the culprits along the way, and now he too is a wanted man, for murder.

In the last scene of that life he is in a saloon, drinking by himself. He drinks too much, feels dizzy, and passes out. When he wakes up he sees himself tied onto the back of a horse but soon realizes he is dead. His soul is now describing the scene, and he learns that some men in the bar gave him poison to knock him out but they gave him too much and he died. He was a wanted man and they were going to turn him in. Mateo's soul guide, Tee, joins our session and answers questions about that past life.

Shelly: What was the purpose of showing Mateo that particular past life?

Tee: He needs to let it go.

Shelly: What lesson did Mateo's soul choose to work on in that past life?

Tee: Anger.

Shelly: Did Mateo's soul complete his lesson with anger?

Tee: No.

Shelly: Did Mateo's soul bring any unresolved karma from that life to his current life?

Tee: Yes, emotional.

Shelly: What can Mateo do to resolve that karma?

Tee: Stop fightting his emotions. Acceptance.

Shelly: What is the source of Mateo's need to constantly wash his hands?

Tee: Not letting go of the fact he was poisoned.

Shelly: What is the source of Mateo's need to constantly check and lock doors?

Tee: Feeling he wasn't there to secure and protect them (his family).

Comfort of Familiar Faces

My clients (and I, myself) have found comfort in realizing that certain people in our current lives have been with us in past lives as well. The role or gender of that person was usually different than the role or gender today. For instance, it can be very comforting to realize the soul of your beloved, deceased mother existed in a prior life as your sister. When I have a client in a past life scene and they are with someone they feel very happy with, or unhappy with, I will ask my client to "look into the face and eyes of that person and tell me if you recognize their *soul* as anyone in your current life today." Usually there is recognition, but not always.

A client, Grace, was in a past life scene as a woman in a small prison cell because she was accused of being a witch due to her use of plants and herbs for medicinal purposes. She was alone in the cell but in this particular scene there was a woman sitting outside her cell, a friend who came to comfort her. Grace recognized the soul of this woman as one of her daughters in her current life.

I have experienced many of my own past life sessions with the help of other past life regression therapists. In one particular session, I recognized the souls of that past life's son and daughter as the same souls of two siblings in my current life. In another past life, I recognized the souls of my two children as the same souls of my current-life children. And yet in another regression, I saw my past life husband's soul as one of my current-life brothers.

In my current life I am the oldest of eight children; therefore, odds are rather high that I have had past lives with several of my siblings. When a client recognizes a soul in a past life as someone in their current life, more than likely they are members of the same soul group. Most of us belong to a soul group made up of ten to twenty souls. As a soul group, we tend to incarnate together over and over again but we take on different roles and genders in the various lifetimes as all of our souls are working on different lessons for our soul evolution. Soul groups are discussed in Chapter 9.

Fear of Death

Years ago, a client, Malia, reached out to me when she had a sudden sense of fearing death. She had no idea why this fear abruptly appeared. When we concluded the session, she had a strong sense of *calm* because she realized her current life wasn't all there is, it wasn't the end, there was much more: past lives, future lives, a soul realm, connection to other souls, guidance, and she was loved unconditionally.

Another client, Paul, had a similar story—he constantly feared losing his wife and children. Paul was financially successful in his current life and, in fact, was prosperous in the past life we visited as well. But visiting the past life still didn't provide an explanation as to why he feared losing his spouse and children.

When his soul guide joined our session I asked, "Where is the source of that fear? Another past life?" His guide said, "Yes," and proceeded to show Paul the source scene. Paul then described himself as a man in that previous life, sitting in a restaurant with his wife and children.

Suddenly, several men burst into the restaurant and took his wife and children. The scene was over quickly but my client learned the details of what unfolded: the wife and children were taken and killed because the man owed money to someone powerful and he had not paid the debt. This was certainly an unpleasant scene to experience, but it helped my client understand why he feared losing his family in his current life.

Appreciating Simple Lives

People who have not experienced a past life regression oftentimes think about past lives as being on the spectacular side, like visiting a past where they were someone in a lofty position of power, or a knight who fought in many battles, or a martyr who stood up for the rights of the underprivileged. Ironically, a vast majority of my client sessions entail visiting past lives that are quite simple in nature, yet still provide very noteworthy messages or provide awareness and clarity about something important.

Reconnecting with Nature

Some clients have seen past lives where they spent much time in nature, walking through forests and feeling so peaceful and connected to the trees, clean air, and water. During these scenes my clients convey the feeling of true comfort, peace, and the beautiful experience of being connected with the Earth. The simple message from these sessions has been to remind my clients of how important it is to spend time in nature in order to relax and have time to reconnect with themselves. Our society is very fast paced and filled with distractions. Cell phones, computers, and televisions keep us continually connected to social media, computer games, and a barrage of negative news. Technology offers tremendous benefits by keeping us connected with family and friends and having access to learning opportunities that would otherwise be expensive and difficult. However, maintaining a balance among electronics, connectivity, and nature is important. My clients are reminded of this when necessary.

My major purpose of facilitating past life regression work is to identify the source of life blockages and to remove them in order to move forward in life with ease and grace. Whether the intention of a past life regression is for healing or curiosity, I have found the results of these sessions often bring a sense of calm to my clients. We will now delve further into past life regressions.

CHAPTER 6

How a Past Life Regression Works

"The client usually gets exactly what they are looking for—for instance, clarity on why they face certain challenges . . ."

I n this chapter I discuss brain wave states, hypnosis, and how a past life regression works. Since I use hypnosis to facilitate past life regressions, I explore brain wave states to facilitate understanding hypnosis. Many of my clients admit to certain anxiety, fear, and hesitation about hypnosis; therefore, I discuss this in much detail to dispel any worries about the process.

Brain Wave States

Below are four brain wave states in which we humans spend various amounts of time during each day:

Beta—Our active state and where we function most of the day. The beta state is associated with the alert mind, which is often working and thinking. This is the brain wave state my clients are in when they arrive at my office and when we converse at the beginning of their session. This is the state clients return to before they leave my office after a session.

Alpha—A relaxed state where brain waves start to slow down, leaving the thinking mind. In alpha we feel more calm, peaceful, and grounded. We often find ourselves in an alpha state during light meditation, after a yoga class, during a walk in the woods, or during any activity that helps to relax the body and mind. This is the brain wave state my clients enter into for a past life regression.

Theta—A drowsy state where the verbal/thinking mind transitions to a deeper state of awareness with stronger intuition. Most of us enter this state during deep meditation. This is the brain wave state my clients enter into during a between life regression.

⋘

Delta—An unconscious state. Monks who have been meditating for decades can reach this state quickly but most of us reach this final state during deep, dreamless sleep. This is the brain wave state that specially trained regression therapists will use when it is important to have their client in an unconscious state in order to access memories the subconscious mind will normally block, such as memories of visitations with extra-terrestrial beings.

⋘

As you are reading or listening to this book, you are most likely in the beta brain wave state: alert, talking, reading, listening, and thinking.

Hypnosis

Hypnosis is the tool I use to facilitate a past life regression. Here are a few facts about the hypnosis I use:

➤ I literally do not hypnotize people; instead, I facilitate clients to hypnotize themselves. All hypnosis is self-hypnosis.

⁂ People will not say or do anything under hypnosis that they don't want to say or do.

⁂ My clients are in full control of their physical, mental, and emotional state during hypnosis. My clients are never under my control.

⁂ Whether in the alpha or theta brain wave state, my clients are aware of what is going on around them (e.g., sounds, room temperature, needing to use the restroom).

⁂ Clients typically remember their session details quite vividly.

I use the sound of my voice and suggested meditative breathing exercises to help my clients relax from the beta state down to the alpha state. The alpha state is similar to how you feel just before you nod off to sleep at night. If you are in bed and about to go to sleep (the alpha state) and you suddenly hear the neighbor's dog bark, your brain will recognize the neighbor's dog is barking but you won't do anything about it. Your body does not stir, you don't think about it, you simply know what you heard and you lay still, ready for sleep.

This is a good description of what my clients feel

like when they are hypnotized to the alpha state. And it's in the alpha brain wave state where my clients can access past life memories.

The next lower brain wave state, theta, is the level I use for clients during a between life regression. I briefly describe this type of regression at the end of this book in Chapter 13.

An acquaintance of mine told me he had a past life regression twenty years ago. He mentioned a few details of the session he had, and then admitted to me he thought it was just his imagination, not truly a past life regression. I then asked him, "Do you remember everything vividly from that session, all of the details from the past life you visited?"

He responded, "Oh, yes." I said, "If you made up that session with your imagination, you would not have remembered all of those details so clearly to this day. Our imagination is not very good at re-membering things we make up." When we imagine things, we have to work at remembering the details. But when we experience an actual event or scene, then we don't have to work at remembering the details, as they are encoded in our memory.

For example, if you were walking on the sidewalk and witnessed a fender bender close by, it is more than likely you would not have to work at remembering the details of what you saw because that scene is imprinted in your memory. On the other hand, if you made up the fender bender, then you would have to work at remembering the made-up details.

Typical Concerns about Hypnosis

If my client has never been hypnotized before, I spend several minutes discussing the hypnosis process because I find that many people are actually nervous about it. Following are several reasons why people may be nervous about hypnosis:

"What if I cannot be hypnotized?" This is a common concern and I assure my client that it is easier to get hypnotized than most people think. In fact, I use a very light level of hypnosis. This is where I explain the multiple brain-wave states, and I begin by describing the beta brain-wave state because that is the state we are in while having this particular discussion. I then explain the alpha state, which is sufficient for my client to access his or her past life memories. I have had many clients mention after their session that their mind was very alert but their arms felt too heavy to lift.

✿

"I don't think I can be hypnotized." I typically respond to this statement with a strong affirmation: "I believe you will do just fine, I am not worried." This is normally enough to help them feel confident, but if not then I repeat a popular saying, "When you think you can or you can't, you are right." I also remind them that the level of hypnosis used is very light. In fact, I have had several clients who have just finished a very good, productive session, and then they look at me and ask, "Was I really hypnotized?" Yes, they were hypnotized but most people feel very, very relaxed.

✿

"I'm nervous about saying or doing something I don't want to." Ironically, many people say this based on their experience seeing stage shows with professional hypnotists who are known to invite many people onto a stage, hypnotize them, and proceed to have those people do a plethora of silly things in order to make the audience laugh. Those people up on stage doing silly things *WANT* to be on stage doing silly things! I assure my clients they will never say or do anything under hypnosis that they do not wish to. In one session with a client, I asked a question about the scene and my client's response was, "It's

personal." The client happened to be my son and there was obviously something he didn't want to share with me, *his mom*. I said, "Okay," and moved on to the next question about the scene.

✿

"I am scared of visiting a past life that is traumatic." Connected to this, the same person typically has the additional worry of coming out of the regression experience with more trauma than healing. This is a common concern for clients who are with me to work on some sort of phobia or fear, such as fear of water. *Our soul guides are responsible for the entire regression; neither I nor the client has any control as to which past life will be visited.* Our soul guides love us completely and everything they do is for our highest good. With that said, I tell my clients that their soul guide knows them well and will not present anything harmful to them. I have witnessed many occasions during which a client's soul guide did not have my client experience the horrible details of a scene; instead, she or he was taken to a time directly after the traumatic event. One example is a client, Sofia, who visited a past life as a seventeen-year-old girl who had just been raped. Sofia's soul guide did not deem it necessary for her to recall the details of

the actual rape; instead, her guide took her to a scene shortly afterward in which she briefly recalled the emotional and physical pain, which were important for her to experience during that session. Sofia's story is further discussed in Chapter 12. Your soul guide knows what you can and cannot handle.

☼

"Can I get stuck in a past life?" No, you will not get stuck in a past life—no one ever has to my knowledge. In the alpha state of hypnosis, the client is remembering details from her or his own soul memory, recalling the memory, *not* physically traveling through time and space to the past life.

Major Components of a Past Life Regression Session

When a client enters my office, I motion to them to take a seat in the comfortable recliner I have for my regression clients. The next thing I do is explain to my client how the entire process works and how much time it will take, typically up to two hours. Many of my clients have found me on the Internet or received a reference from a friend; therefore this meeting is usually the first time I have met them. By explaining the entire process, I am giving my client time to feel comfortable in their surroundings and with me, and to start to relax.

The regression process begins with a ten- to fifteen-minute discussion of the questionnaire the client has brought with them (explained below). We then move into the hypnosis and regression that together last about ninety minutes, and then we spend the last five to fifteen minutes of the session processing the experience when the client has returned to an awake state (beta).

I record most of the session and provide the recording to my client afterward. I also take detailed notes; I transcribe these and email them to my clients afterward as well. Though my clients typically remember all details of their session vividly, it's still helpful to listen to the recording at times and to read my notes. I do not transcribe the entire session, just the highlights.

The following sections describe each portion of the regression process in more detail.

Preparation

The first ten to fifteen minutes of a session consist of a two-way discussion between the client and me. Before I meet with my client, I have emailed my client a one-page questionnaire that asks for a basic overview of several areas of my client's life: whether they have had a past life regression before, goals for the session, their relationship history with family and friends, physical/emotional history, fears/phobias, work history, and their spiritual perspective. I do not require a detailed history of their life; I basically want to know about their life at the moment and the major challenges my client is dealing with.

This discussion is important for many reasons, but the most important is that by discussing these items, my client is focusing on his or her intentions to alert their soul guide about what needs to come forward in the upcoming session.

Neither I nor the client has control as to which past life will be visited; the client's soul guide makes that determination. The client usually gets exactly what they are looking for—for instance, clarity on why they face certain challenges such as why their father was abusive, why they fear the dark, or why they have recurrent dreams of being on the Titanic. Sometimes their soul guides bring forward a different experience not obviously connected to a given challenge, but rather one that is more useful overall for the client.

Session Begins

Once we have completed discussing the questionnaire contents, we are ready to start the regression portion of the session. I offer my clients a quick restroom break since they will be in a relaxed state for about 90 minutes. When ready my client will recline the chair to a comfortable position, close their eyes, and prepare for their journey back in time. The process of helping the client get hypnotized and helping them arrive at the first scene of a past life generally takes about seven minutes. I look and listen for cues that indicate when my client has reached the alpha state of hypnosis; I will devote additional time as needed to help my client get to where she or he needs to be. Sometimes I play relaxing, meditative music in the background to help my clients relax. I do not play music if my client is hearing impaired, as music would be disruptive in that case.

Once my client has entered into a past life scene, I begin asking questions about which I wish for my client to respond based on what they see, feel, or sense. How a client speaks during a session often matches their personality when not hypnotized. For example, if a client is normally rather quiet and reserved, then they will be the same during a regression and I typically have to ask a lot of questions to encourage them to share what they are experiencing. In constrast, if a client is very talkative and descriptive by nature, then they tend to be the same during a session without a lot of prompting from me. I ask a lot of questions in the first scene because I wish for my client to feel comfortable and confident that what they are experiencing is normal.

One thing that is different among my clients is how they experience their past life scenes. Some clients will see a scene and provide vivid details, others vaguely see the scene. Some feel like they are in a particular place, yet others describe the scene as if they are watching from a distance, rather than being *in* the scene. Once I can identify how my client experiences the first scene, then I know how to adjust my questions to match their ability to answer. For example, if a client sees things clearly, then I know it's safe to continue asking what they *see* in different scenes. If, however, their experience is more feeling based or if the scene is not clear, then I will ask questions such as, "Where do you feel you are?" or "Who do you feel or sense is around you?" or "Imagine that you reach down to touch the ground. What do you feel—dirt, wood floor, grass?" Some clients pop into a scene quickly, others need time for the scene to become clear to them. During my own past life regressions facilitated by other therapists, I know that scenes come into focus very slowly and my regression therapist needs to give me time before I can describe the scenes clearly.

Past-life Scenes until Death

I typically guide my clients to several important scenes in a past life, progressing from the point they entered that life all the way to the end of that life. Clients also enter past lives at different ages; some enter their first scene as a child, others may be twenty-five or forty-five years old.

In every scene, I will ask them how old they are, where they are, what they are doing, who is around them, and, especially, how they feel emotionally. The emotional question is important because if they feel concerned, scared, sad, or elated, then it's important to find out why. Once we reach the last day of that lifetime, I ask additional questions such as the year, the world region where they spent their life, how they felt about that lifetime, and review their body to determine which part is causing that specific day to be the last in their life.

Soul Guide Visit

When we have concluded visiting the client's past life, I then request my client to silently call forth their soul guide. I wait a moment and then ask my client if they feel or see a presence near them. Most times my clients feel and see their guide.

When I ask my client what having their guide near them feels like, I receive responses such as: "I feel surrounded with a hug", "I feel so loved", "He is so happy to see me". Descriptions of what my clients see when their guides are with them range from vivid details of features such as "She's a Native American woman" to "a vibrant ball of light directly in front of me". When the soul guide is with my client, I take the opportunity to ask their guide many questions we have about the past life visited that have not been answered yet. Details about soul guides are explained in Chapter 7.

Concluding the Session

When I have covered what is necessary for my client, I thank my client's soul guide for their loving support, and then I give my client the opportunity to thank their guide personally. When gratitude expressions are complete, I encourage my client to release all pain and issues associated with that past life, to just let them go and leave them in the past because they don't serve any purpose in their current life.

I then tell my client to return to their awake state as I count to ten. Some clients come back by the time I count to ten, others need an additional minute or two to get reoriented. We then spend five to ten minutes discussing the session. I encourage my client to go home and take time to write in a journal about their experience, and to draw pictures of important scenes if they are so inclined.

A two-hour session goes by very quickly and most clients are amazed that two hours have passed. On some occasions I have heard from clients after their session that they were then able to have vivid dreams of other past lives and some could even start accessing information about their past lives when meditating. For these people, it seems that having a past life regression allowed them to open a portal for their own access to past-life information that they did not have before the session.

Personal Story

Releasing the source of a current life issue:
I had a client, Rowan, who stated he wanted to work

on his anger issues. During the session, my client visited a past life as a young boy, and he is alone with his mother. He was raised by his mother who was very loving and cheerful, but he started to wonder about his father.

His mother never talked about his father, whether good, bad, or indifferent. He didn't know where his father was, and he became very angry about being abandoned by his father; in his early forties in that life he was diagnosed with stomach cancer.

The anger had built up so much that it manifested into cancer and he soon died. At the conclusion of visiting that life, I encouraged my client to release the anger since he had no benefits from it being carried forward into his current life. When I talked with this client three months later, he said seeing the source of his anger really resolved a lot of his anger issues. Before having a session with me, he did not know where the anger was coming from in his life and he would have outbursts that he could not control. Going to the source of the anger allowed him to release it, thereby giving him more discernment and thus control of anger in his current life.

This is a perfect example of a client getting exactly what he was looking for. There are other times when something completely different comes about via the client's soul guide because it's for a higher purpose. Quite possibly there is a bigger issue that the client isn't facing that they need to work on.

CHAPTER 7

Soul Guides

Who Are They?

Soul guides are advanced, benevolent, loving entities who have completed all of their soul lessons on Earth; therefore, they no longer feel the necessity of incarnating on Earth. They have also experienced much training in the soul realm to become a soul guide to other souls such as ourselves. Because they have completed all of their Earth lessons and know how difficult Earth school is, they are highly qualified to help us newer souls navigate. A soul guide was assigned to you when your soul was created from the source of all creation. This entity is always with you from the birth of your soul and onwards; the guide plays an important role throughout our lives. All of us have many other guides, healers, and angels who help and watch over us.

Our soul guides assist us in navigating our Earth incarnations as well as guiding us when we are between lives in the soul realm; various soul guides stay with us until our souls have completed all Earth lessons. Their love is unconditional and they are with us day and night when we are happy or down, when we are doing well in our lives and when we are not. Even during those times we feel abandoned they are still with us. A client, Mary, had experienced many challenges in her current life and felt that her soul guide had not been there to help her during such challenges. At the point during her session when I asked her guide, Rue, questions on her behalf, I then suggested that Mary ask her guide any remaining questions. Mary asked Rue, "Why weren't you there for me during the challenging times in my life when I needed you most?" Her loving guide responded, "Because you fight me. I help you but you push back, you don't allow me to help."

Because our soul guides have guided us, watched over us, and helped us make many decisions, they have grown to know us very well. They know our strengths, weaknesses, and our personalities. They know what lessons we have successfully and unsuccessfully worked on in the past and they help us decide which lessons our upcoming incarnations will entail. Soul guides will not be with our souls forever and they will change out from time to time as our souls develop and advance. Using K-12 as an example, we may have a soul guide who is with us for the beginning portion of our soul evolvement, say K-4, and then they may swap out with a different soul guide when our soul is ready for more advanced lessons and guidance. It is normal to spend ten, twenty, even thirty lifetimes passing through a particular level because there is so much to learn.

I admit that my favorite part of a client's past life session with me is when the client meets their soul guide. It sounds odd to say "when my client meets their soul guide," because in reality, they have known their soul guide for a very, very long time! But in our humanness, we often forget we have guides who are always with us. That veil of amnesia (given to us at each incarnation's birth time) and the busyness of our lives helps us shut off the connection to our divine, loving guides and we forget we are not alone during this venture. The reconnection of my clients with their guides is a loving reunion, and it's at this point during a regression that my clients often get quite emotional, stating that they feel so loved in the presence of their guides.

Here are some examples of how my clients describe meeting with their soul guides for the first time during a session:

I see a light around me, it is a fairy type of entity on my right, by my face. Its energy is female and her name is Flutter.

I feel her presence in front of me. I feel warm and safe with her and her name is Eleanor.
I feel a male presence in front of me; he appears dark purple and tall. I feel happy in his presence, his name is Steph-aw-nee.

Her name is Mary and she is on my right side. I feel warm and safe with her energy. Mary just left and another guide came forward on my left side—his name is Maleeki. His energy feels comforting. Maleeki also leaves and then there is a bright light behind me, it feels masculine and feels like an angel. I feel *strong* with his energy. It is Archangel Michael.

My guide appears and it's my grandfather from my current life. We are to call him Charlie. He is in front of me and he looks happy, healthy, and he feels comforting. There is a long line of people behind him. They are those who came before him, his ancestors, all of us are connected.

I feel his presence, he's moving all around me; he is a hawk, he's big and there is a lot of white around him. I feel safe with him, his name is Paul.

Some clients have recognized their soul guides during a session. I have heard comments such as, "She's familiar, I have met her before," and "I have seen this guide during a meditation."

Soul guides have personalities and they have much patience with us. They have been through these lessons on Earth and they know it may take several lifetimes to complete a single lesson.

Although they do not have to incarnate anymore on Earth, occasionally someone's soul guide will incarnate for a period of time, often to help one of their assigned souls on their Earthly path. My client, Rowan, met his soul guide during a session and recognized him as his younger brother in his current life. At the end of his session when we were discussing the regression details, I asked Rowan what his younger brother is like today. His response was, "He's wise beyond his years."

That answer didn't surprise me since his brother's soul is very advanced. When a soul guide incarnates on Earth to help one or more in their assigned group, it does not mean they are missing in the soul realm or leaving the rest of their group unattended. When a soul guide incarnates on Earth, they only bring a portion of their soul with them into the body, as the rest of their soul stays in the soul realm. In fact, all of us typically leave a large portion of our soul in the soul realm and that portion is referred to as our higher self. Our physical bodies cannot handle 100 percent of our soul; it's too much energy for a physical body to contain. We can and do function well with a portion of our soul such as 80 percent or 60 percent or even less. This is discussed further in Chapter 9, Soul Groups.

Upon the creation of each new soul, most of us are assigned to a soul guide. I say "most of us" because there are some exceptions, which are discussed in Chapter 8, Soul Types. Our new souls are also grouped with several other new souls into a soul group that stays together and incarnates over and over again on Earth.

Have you ever experienced a very difficult time in your life when you believed the only reason you made it through was that you felt some sort of unseen guidance or support? What I mean by "guidance or support" is that you felt there was some invisible, benevolent entity or being who you felt was by your side, enveloping you in unconditional love and helping you feel supported. Whether we call this entity God, soul guide, guardian angel, divine spirit, or higher self, all are correct because we always have this loving support around us. In this book I refer to soul guides as the specific entity that works with us in our day-to-day lives as we maneuver the challenges associated with the lesson we chose to work on and the circumstances to facilitate our work on that lesson. Our guides were present to help us select the appropriate lesson we were ready to sign up for in each lifetime and they stay with us to guide us along our path for each lifetime.

When I was growing up, I encountered many

challenges. During such times, I would lie in my bed at night and often felt that I wasn't alone, as if some benevolent being or group of beings was watching over me. I tended to think it was a group of guardian angels. I could never see or hear them; it was just a feeling. God, angels, or soul guides never leave our side but we often forget their presence. Other times we block them as Mary did in the example a few paragraphs above.

Higher Self Also a Guide

When we incarnate into our bodies, we do not bring 100 percent of our soul into our body because it's too much energy. A portion of our soul stays in the soul realm and this portion then acts as our higher self. Our higher self guides us as well. Our higher self in the soul realm does not have an ego like that of our human selves; therefore, the guidance from our higher self (like the guidance from our soul guides) will always come from a loving, heart-centered perspective.

Why Are They Here?

Our soul guides are here to guide us throughout our soul's evolvement. As new, beginner souls we experience many lessons in the soul realm before we are ready to begin incarnating on Earth. Picture your new soul going through several basic lessons in the soul realm, possibly learning about energy, love, light, and communication. Now your soul is ready to embark for lessons on Earth, incarnating as a human and selecting lessons to work on. As new souls, we are not able to make decisions on our own on how to proceed; therefore, our assigned soul guide is there to help us. As beginner-level souls ready to come and go from the Earth school, our soul guide will guide us to the appropriate lessons to start off with. Using the K-12 example does not suggest that we will experience only thirteen lessons/lifetimes on earth (one for each K-12 grade) because, as mentioned previously, it's likely we spend many, many lifetimes getting through the basic kindergarten level of life lessons. The basic topics to be learned in kindergarten can be akin to the basic lessons for a new soul such as learning to love yourself, having love for others, or learning to be comfortable in a physical body in Earth's dense environment.

As we attend our kindergarten class, our teacher provides guidance and learning as we proceed through basic beginner lessons, and this is similar to what our soul guides do for us. Our soul guides have in-depth knowledge of our souls and understand the lessons we have worked on and how we have fared with each of those lessons; therefore, they are highly skilled in guiding us further. They also help us understand when we did not complete a lesson and need a do-over.

Soul guides have complete, gentle, and unrestricted love for us. They help us decide which lesson we are going to work on every time we prepare to enter into our next incarnation. And when we mess up in a lifetime—don't do a lesson or don't complete it—, they don't judge us. It's more like, "I know that was a tough lesson but here are some things you can work on while in the soul realm to help you prepare for taking on that lesson again in your next incarnation." They understand the lessons can be quite tough, and it often takes many lifetimes to complete one specific lesson.

They frequently guide us to work on other things in between lives and possibly in future incarnations to help us prepare for taking on the incomplete lesson again. For example, if a soul chooses *responsibility* as their life lesson but doesn't do well with that lesson, their soul guide might recommend that their next lifetime be dedicated to working on a different lesson such as independence in order to better prepare the soul for returning to the lesson of responsibility. When your soul completes a difficult life on Earth and returns to the soul realm, picture your loving soul guide there to greet you, putting their loving arms around your shoulders, welcoming you back, commenting on your difficult Earth life, and then suggesting that the two of you will review and work on the results together.

Do you ever have that gut feeling about something such as making a decision in your life when dealing with a challenge or which route to take to work? For example, when you want to go your usual route to the store, but you get a nagging feeling to take a different route? That is your soul guide nudging you. It can also be your higher self guiding you, or a combined effort.

A simple example is Stacey who arrived several minutes late to my metaphysics class. When I was discussing this topic during the lecture, Stacey's eyes lit up and she shared an experience on her way to class. As she was driving her normal route to the building, she had a nagging feeling that she should turn onto a different street, but ignored it. On her normal route, she encountered road construction that then required her to follow several detours, causing her to be late.

When we pick a lesson or purpose for an upcoming incarnation and we choose the challenges and opportunities for that life, we often go off track. In fact, we typically weave on and off our path. When we go off track, our guides continue to guide us, talking in our ear, giving us that gut feeling to guide us back on track.

We can choose to listen or not, and we can return to our path, and then we'll go off course again at some point. Meanwhile they are always guiding us back to our chosen path.

Soul guides drive the entire past-life regression session with my clients. Once again, my client's soul guides know their students completely and will bring the past lives and information forward that will be the most beneficial for my clients.

What Do Soul Guides Look Like?

Every client has a different experience with how their guides appear to them during a regression. Some clients can see them vividly and proceed to describe their features to me. One client described her guide who appeared as a Native American woman with a long braid down her back along with a bow slung over her shoulder and even noted the bow and arrow represented strength. She was wearing a beautiful dress made of animal skin.

Other clients don't see vivid images; instead, they describe a beautiful, bright light, and even describe its color and the position of the light—in front of them, to their left, above and all around, and so on. Guides present themselves in various forms as they know our personalities. The guides know what my client needs to experience and they present themselves accordingly.

My own guide appeared to me as a black oval with a bright light right in the center. As much as I would have loved to see my guide with vivid, human-like features, instead, I saw a simple image. What mattered most is that he was there and I was able to feel his energy and hear his guidance for me.

When a client's soul guide comes forward, I ask my client where the guide is positioned in relation to them and how they appear. I also ask whether they can feel the energy from their guide as being mas-culine, feminine, or androgynous (combined). Soul guides often have a masculine or feminine energy that my clients can sense. Sometimes the client cannot discern masculine or feminine energy—it's more androgynous. My own guide has masculine energy.

Some guides have appeared to my clients in animal form. One client's guide came forward as a dark grey wolf and another client's was a mountain lion. Soul guides will present themselves in whatever form they know will resonate with my client and in whatever form will not distract from the session itself. What matters most about a session is the information that is provided and not how pretty the images are.

Names

Soul guides have names. At the time during a client session when their soul guide comes forward, I ask the guide what name they would like to be called during the session. Most of the time they answer with a specific name; this is helpful for me as I direct my questions to the guide on my client's behalf.

On the few occasions when we do not get an answer regarding the name, I will ask more questions such as, "Is your name a vibration or a frequency that my client is unable to understand in their current human form?" Sometimes the answer is "yes," and my client then feels relieved that our question is not being ignored. If this is not the response, then I ask whether the guide can spell the name for us. I have found this to be quite helpful when my client has said, "I'm having a difficult time understanding the name." Sometimes the name is very unique and I have to guess the spelling; other times it's a common Earth name. To name a few, I have heard Ashtar, Elma, George, Michael, Rue, Nova, and even Archangel Michael.

Gretchen's soul guide appeared as a large black bird and told us his name was Amos. Now Amos knew Gretchen's personality and when she asked him a question about a situation in her current life that had carried over from a prior life, Amos replied, "Get over it!"

And then he flew away. Gretchen actually laughed at the response. Based on Gretchen's response to the message from Amos, I had a feeling Amos had been telling her soul to get over it for a long time. Again, our guides know our personalities and they will present themselves in ways that resonate with us.

My own soul guide's name was difficult to pronounce in a way I could understand, so my facilitator asked to spell it and he provided "Me-et." I knew there were more letters that followed but the first few were sufficient to let us carry on with the session.

How Can You Reach Your Soul Guide?

Our guides want to help us as much as possible and they are delighted when we ask them for guidance. One thing I do in each of my client sessions is to ask the client's guide this direct question: "What can [client's name] do when they want or need to reach you?" Though I can easily tell my client how to reach their guides at any time, I find it more beneficial for my client to hear it directly from their soul guide. The guide always provides an answer directly to my client (which they repeat for my benefit) and the most common answer is, "Just ask. I'm always there."

The next most common answer to this question is, "Meditate or be still, then you will have my attention." This is important because we humans get busy. The third most common response is, "Go out into nature, you'll find me there." When you go out into nature and put your phone away—you are away from your TV, your computer, and your *stuff*—THEN you can get in touch with nature's tranquil energy, which is easily connected to the soul realm and our guides. You don't even have to ask for guidance out loud. All communication in the soul realm is telepathic; therefore, they hear you even if you silently present the question.

In our busy human lives, it is easy for us to forget that we have a loving soul guide who is always there, watching, guiding, and offering help. We forget to *ask* for their help. It's also easy to think we are bothering them, asking too much, or we feel reluctant to ask them.

Just ask—they are here to serve you! But they are not going to force their help on you. They cannot force you into any sort of thought or action because part of our agreement for being human is to have free will within our own lives. It's also not useful to ask them fortune-telling types of questions, such as "When am I going to make a million dollars?" or "When am I going to meet my perfect life partner?" But they are very willing to help with questions such as, "I need your guidance in this messy situation with my business partner" and "Please provide me guidance in how to deal with my teenage son."

The irony in asking for guidance is that our soul guides often answer us more than once but we humans are quite adept at ignoring or discounting the guidance when it does come! It helps to add this to your request: "Please provide your guidance in a manner that is very clear to me so that I understand it." It's important to then pay attention for the answer.

The answer may come to you during your sleep state, during meditation, or even when you are stopped at a traffic light on your way home from work the next day.

An excellent book regarding asking for guidance is *E-Squared: Nine Do-It-Yourself Energy Experiments That Prove Your Thoughts Create Your Reality* by Pam Grout. I attended a workshop with Pam where I learned of the books she wrote, which I then bought and read. Not long afterwards, I had a family situation that had my heart twisted in knots: a young nephew and his two younger sisters were taken away from their parents and put into foster care. They lived several hundred miles from me and I didn't know what to do. Should I hire an attorney and get involved? Should I jump in and try to get custody of the kids? Who were they living with? Were they together or separated?

So many questions clouded my mind. I decided to follow one of the exercises in Pam's book: ask for guidance in this situation, give my request a time limit, and ask for the response to be very clear for me. Well, the next day as I was driving home from work, I was stopped at a traffic light and I suddenly got a strong message in my mind, "Get your ego out of the way." I thought about that message for a moment and my mind suddenly started to declutter from all the ego-based thoughts and I knew my new direction in the matter: Assess the situation first, get in touch with the foster parents (I was given their names), observe the situation for a while, and then decide what to do. I did get in touch with the foster parents and I established a nice relationship with them. A month later I traveled to visit the kids and found that they were thriving in their foster home. After fifteen months the kids were reunited with their mother. I am glad I listened to the guidance that was given to me and I got my ego out of the way.

Ask for guidance from your guides and *listen* for the answer. You still get to choose whether to follow the guidance. They want to be of service to you. Remember those gut feelings you have? Think of the times you have been at the crossroads with a situation and you had to make a decision, and one decision felt right and the other decision did not. Your soul guide was there, helping to guide you.

Young children are very in tune with their soul guides and other spiritual beings around them. Until about age five or six, kids are very connected. When they tell you stories of the imaginary friend who sits next to them while playing or at the dinner table, there's a good chance it's their soul guide. Kids can see and communicate with them because the veil at this time in their lives is very thin. I am confident many of you can remember interesting things that your young children, nieces/nephews, or grandchildren have said to support this. When children enter school, the veil tends to get thicker due to pressure from others to stop believing in imaginary playmates.

All of us have been with our guides for a very, very long time but as we are born into our human incarnations, we often enter this world with amnesia about the soul realm. Having a regression session often lifts the veil enough for my client to gain confidence that this single life is not all there is. A session is a very special reunion for many reasons:

- ✿ My client gets to remember firsthand that they really do have a guide.

- ✿ After meeting and conversing with their guide during the session, my client understands their guide is always there for them.

- ✿ Finally, my client learns they have the ability to call upon their guide whenever they need or wish to do so.

I often recommend meditation for my clients to help develop a communication channel to their guides. Now meditation doesn't always have to be sitting quietly in the lotus position on the floor. There are many ways to meditate.

Walking, gardening, hiking, riding your bike, star gazing, sitting comfortably with soft music playing, or washing dishes are all ways to meditate. Anything that can get your mind into a quiet zone is a form of meditation.

The key is to find what works for you. Many people have difficulty turning off their monkey mind, that is, the busy part of your mind which sometimes does not want to turn off or turn down. Some people do better with guided meditations and there are many free options on YouTube, while others do better with soft music.

By slowing down our minds, we are able to elevate our frequency, which then enables us to tune into our guides and their guidance. My advice about meditation is to find what works for you and simply do it. Five minutes a day is better than nothing. Just like yoga, we are never perfect at it; we're always practicing.

How Do We Know When We Are Getting the Right Guidance?

We know when we are getting guidance from our soul guides and our higher self when it *feels* right, in our heart and gut. Guidance from the soul realm always comes from a loving, accepting, and forgiving perspective, and never from a perspective of payback or revenge. That's how you can tell if it's the right guidance. Sometimes our logical minds have a difficult time with this guidance because our ego and pride often get in the way of wanting to listen to the heartfelt answer or advice.

Exercise

The intention of this exercise is for you to con-sider any evidence that you have met, seen, or felt the presence of your soul guide.

1. Have you ever met your guide?

2. Do your dreams include a loving entity who visits you?

3. Does your guide have a feminine, masculine, or combined (androgynous) energy?

4. Do you have a name for your guide?

5. Have you ever felt your guide's presence while awake or in meditation?

6. Is there an area of your home where you feel their presence more than other places?

7. Do you feel their presence in nature more than elsewhere?

NOTES:

_____

_____

_____

_____

_____

_____

_____

_____

_____

_____

_____

_____

_____

_____

_____

CHAPTER 8

Soul Types

All of us are eternal souls and our souls can be identified as being one of two types:

Earth souls—These souls have spent most or all of their incarnations on planet Earth and feel very comfortable on this plane. In fact, Earth souls tend to not think anything is out of the ordinary about being in a physical body, eating the food, and drinking the water here; it feels normal for us.

❦

Interplanetary souls—These souls have spent most of their incarnations elsewhere, such as another planet, a star, or in a different galaxy. Interplanetary souls come from advanced civilizations and have been coming to Earth to incarnate into human form in order to share the gifts they bring from their home places. Although these souls have been coming to Earth for eons, they are now coming to Earth in greater numbers because, quite frankly, we need their help! They are here to help elevate and enlighten humanity, our frequency, and our human consciousness.

I am an Earth soul and I feel very connected and comfortable in the Earth realm. Confirmation for my soul type was given during my own between life regression with another regression therapist. I have no allergies and I have never had any feelings of discomfort being in my physical body.

In contrast, interplanetary souls often have challenges. Although they come into being just like Earth souls (conceived, born, and growing up in families like the rest of us), many of these souls are from other places that are not as dense as the Earth plane. And this is the reason many interplanetary souls have issues being on Earth.

For their Earthly incarnations, Interplanetary souls also choose lessons to work on and script their lives, just like Earth souls. Even though their souls are from advanced civilizations, they still need to go through the Earth school of learning in order to integrate and be a part of humanity.

Unique Gifts of Interplanetary Souls

All of us come into our incarnations with gifts to share. But Interplanetary souls come to Earth with unique gifts to share because they come from more advanced places. When I am with a client who learns they are an Interplanetary soul, one of the follow-up questions to their soul guide is, "What gift did my client bring from their home place to share on Earth?" Following is a shortlist of responses I have heard over the years.

- ✿ Artwork, creativity, and ability to connect with people in a warm and loving way, to ease their fears.

- ✿ How to be happy, stay centered, and stay loving no matter what.

- ✿ Healing.

- ✿ Happiness.

- ✿ Hope, freedom, freedom from evil, and freedom from negativity.

✪ To seed the Earth. This was needed as her home planet receded (faded) away. Earth is a hospitable place for many souls.

✪ Healing. Follow the path of all interests, both old and new.

✪ Wisdom of communication without words, particularly on how to heal—you just know how to heal people. To help you remember this gift, take some classes from alternative places, locally. You will feel joy and excitement when you are on the right path.

✪ The same brightness as from the star you come from; its sparkle and magic.

✪ The ability to communicate in a way that reaches some people deeply and changes them.

✪ Love and joy help people connect; she's a catalyst.

✪ Understanding.

✪ Acceptance and love.

✪ Happiness and love.

Importance of Knowing Your Soul Type

When one reflects on the foundational concept seven in Chapter 4 about challenges in our lives, it's difficult enough going through life with the challenges we have scripted. But if you are an Interplanetary soul, then it's likely you have a list of *additional* challenges you must deal with. These challenges often act as blocks that have held you back from enjoying a fulfilling and happy life.

After reading this chapter, many of you will have a good idea which type of soul you are. A majority of my clients are Interplanetary souls. They are often the ones seeking answers to the many questions and feelings they have endured for most of their lifetimes.

Signs of Interplanetary Souls

What is interesting about Interplanetary souls is that they frequently have symptoms or traits that can help them realize who they are. Some of the more common traits follow.

- ✿ Allergic to many things on Earth: plants, foods, animals, chemicals, food additives

- ✿ Growing up feeling homesick

- ✿ Never feeling like they fit in with groups

of people (including family of origin)

✹ Not understanding human thinking

✹ Feeling very comforted by star gazing

✹ Difficulty connecting easily with people

✹ Empathic, sometimes to an extreme

✹ Not feeling like they belong here (on Earth)

✹ Difficulty feeling connected to and comfortable in their bodies

✹ Often wear unique clothing and hairstyles

✹ Frequent vivid dreams of places not associated with Earth and/or very ancient or future times on Earth

✹ Strong interest in books, documentaries, and movies about extraterrestrial beings or aliens

✹ Have experienced visitations from ETs

When I bring up the topic of soul types during my speaking engagements and workshops, I always see the "Aha!" look on a few faces. It's as if the light-bulb was finally turned on as to why they have felt so out of place for their entire lives, or the now-*that*-explains-why-I-am-the-way-I-am(!) expression on their faces.

I am delighted when these people stay after the engagement to talk with me and get more information. There are many resources now available to help them learn more about themselves and to live more comfortably in the Earth realm. A few of these resources are listed in Recommended Readings in the Appendix.

Earth Is Dense

Earth is considered a very dense and heavy planet. Observe the table your computer is sitting on, or the walls in the room you are in, or the feeling of your finger tapping on your thigh. These are all very hard, dense items made up of matter. Some of the places where Interplanetary souls come are not this dense.

If you consider the skin around your human body as being a type of "container" for your soul, then consider an Interplanetary soul who comes from a place where it did not live inside a container or have dense, physical bodies as we have on Earth. Instead, their soul existed as a collection of energy that was free-flowing and could change shape and size on a whim, it could possibly change colors too. Or perhaps their soul was integrated as a wisp of smoke, or an essence, or a ball of light—no density, no thick matter.

When Interplanetary souls come into the Earth environment, some have difficulty getting accustomed to being in the physical container of a body. It's hard for some of them to feel connected to their bodies on Earth. Some Interplanetary souls are challenged with being in physical form and that in and of itself acts as a block to Interplanetary souls living on Earth and sharing their gifts. Besides possibly carrying unresolved karma forward to their current lives, Interplanetary souls have the additional obstacles of physical/emotional blocks derived from being integrated into physical bodies on Earth.

Consider what Earth's inhabitants do to agriculture and farm animals to ensure profits and quantity over quality. Pesticides, chemical fertilizers, vaccines, genetically modified organisms, pollution—all of these things can cause Interplanetary souls to be ultrasensitive and sometimes allergic to our food, water, and environment.

Humans Are Dense

If you look at history and humankind, it's easy to see

that a large proportion of humanity is not loving or kind to others. We are constantly reminded of this during newscasts: wars, genocide, drug rings, human trafficking, corruption, and so much more. We often have strife in our own interpersonal relationships with friends, family, and inconsiderate drivers on the road.

One client in her mid-twenties named Heather came in for a session. From our discussion at the beginning, I figured she was an Earth soul—no allergies, comfortable with her body and her life.

During the session when I asked her soul guide if her soul was an Earth or Interplanetary soul, I was a bit surprised to hear "Interplanetary." She was surprised too and did not know what this meant, but I assured her we would discuss the topic thoroughly at the end of the session. I also asked her guide how many lifetimes she had experienced on Earth and the response was "579." No wonder she didn't have any difficulties on Earth as an Interplanetary soul; she had lived many lifetimes on Earth and had become accustomed to its dense environment.

At the end of her session when I discussed Interplanetary souls, Heather recalled something interesting she said after seeing an unpleasant news clip on TV several weeks earlier. She blurted out to her boyfriend, "I just don't get these humans!" When she realized what she said, she was confused as to why she would say such a thing, as if she was not part of humanity. *NOW* it made sense to her.

Empaths

Most Interplanetary souls are empaths. Empaths are people who are very sensitive to their environment and the energy around them, and especially human energy. Empaths can absorb the energy of people around them like a sponge, and this is not good if the energy is negative.

Some empaths understand this and know how to protect themselves from the negative energy of people and things around them. Other empaths do not understand this and carry a lot of heaviness via depression and anxiety. Fortunately, many books and other resources (see below) are now available to help empaths learn about their challenges and how to deal with them.

What Interplanetary Souls Can Do

Realizing they are Interplanetary souls allows people to identify the blocks in their lives, how to reduce or remove those blocks, and then proceed with sharing their gifts with humanity. Their gifts include healing energy, healing arts, creative arts, psychic abilities, sound or light healing, or shining the light of love and happiness with others.

I ask my clients' soul guides what they can do to reduce or remove many of the blocks in their lives. Following are the most common responses.

- ✪ To feel more connected to their bodies: meditate, spend more time in nature, swim

- ✪ To heal certain physical ailments: eat healthier, remove sugar, do yoga, exercise

- ✪ To reconnect with their guides and higher self: meditate, spend time in nature

Interplanetary souls need to identify their allergies so that they can take appropriate measures to remove those things from their diet and environment. If you are an empath, learn how to protect yourself. An excellent resource is *The Empath's Survival Guide* by Judith Orloff, MD, an an empath herself. If you suspect your child is an empath, other excellent books include *The Children of Now*, by Meg Blackburn Losey, PhD, and *The Indigo Children: The New Kids Have Arrived*, by Lee Carroll and Jan Tober.

Exercise

1. Do you believe you are an Earth
    or Interplanetary soul?

2. What characteristics about
    you support your belief?

CHAPTER 9

Soul Groups

A soul group is a collection of ten to twenty souls who are grouped together at the moment of their creation. When your soul is created, it is assigned to a soul group. As a group, you and the others will incarnate together on Earth over and over again. Each member in the group takes on different lessons, roles, and challenges, but you stay together. You and your soul group members agree on which roles each of you will take in your next incarnations together as you help one another work on your respective chosen lessons.

In one incarnation, you may choose to be the mother of another group member and that soul agrees to be your daughter. In yet another incarnation, the two of you may agree to be siblings, or husband and wife, or grandfather and grandson. Though the group tends to evolve together, each member evolves on their own path and not all members stay at the exact same level of soul evolvement. Some members work on one group of lessons while others may work on a different group of lessons, and then there are others who experience do-overs. One group member may complete the lesson of self-love in one incarnation whereas it might take another soul group member three (or more) lifetimes to complete the same lesson.

What Do Members of a Soul Group Look Like?

Most often a between life regression (Chapter 13) includes my client meeting with the members of their soul group. Sometimes the members of the group appear to my client with actual features and look similar to their physical form on Earth. Other times my clients describe their members as looking like light or a ball of energy emitting a particular color. Regardless of whether my client can see specific features or not, my client recognizes the energy from each one and can immediately name who the members are.

The first time I met with my soul group, the

members first appeared in the distance in front of me and they looked like white lights. They were bopping up and down when they saw me and I intuitively knew who they were because they were excited to see me in this realm. As I approached them, my soul merged with theirs and together we started swirling in a circle as they were helping me get acclimated to their frequency. After a few moments when we finished the circle, I was able to see each soul as they came forward one by one. The group had split into two smaller groups with one being close to me and the other moving into the background. I was to only meet with the members of the closer group during that session, not with the other group.

The members of the close group were my husband, son, daughter, father, mother, and youngest brother. The first two souls to approach me were my husband and son and they were acting funny which made me chuckle. What does "acting funny" look like? My husband's soul had his shirt unbuttoned so I would recognize it was him with his hairy chest. I said, "I know it's you, silly!" My son's soul was wearing a long, white robe and his hair was crafted as gold ringlets around his face. I knew he was showing off his soul colors of white and gold, indicators of an advanced being. Souls have personalities and I got the distinct impression my group liked to have fun. Next, I noticed my youngest brother's soul—he appeared dark and a bit smaller than the others. My regression therapist asked me why he appeared that way and the answer was, "He feels bad for what he did" (suicide). Two other members of my group appeared smaller than the rest and I learned it was because their souls joined our group later and were younger souls than the rest of us.

Can We Visit Incarnate Soul Group Members?

Excepting my brother, all of the souls I just mentioned in my soul group were still living. When members of your soul group are still incarnate on Earth with you, the reason you can visit with them in the soul realm is because you are meeting with their higher self. The higher self is that portion of their soul that stays in the soul realm even when they are incarnate on Earth.

The portion of the soul left in the soul realm as the higher self does not affect their visit with my clients, whether it's 20 percent (the other 80 percent is in the body on Earth) or 100 percent (their soul is not incarnate on Earth at the time).

Members of your soul group who have passed away on Earth will be there too. Whether these souls have reincarnated already or not, the higher self portion of their soul will be there to greet you. Typically, the members who preceded you to the soul realm in your current life will stay there for a long time (human time) until the rest of your soul group joins them in the soul realm, at which point your group decides on the next incarnation to do together.

How Do They Act?

The souls in your group are very loving and happy when you visit them in the soul realm because there is only unconditional love and light energy there. Their higher selves are very loving and accepting of my clients regardless of how their human self is behaving on Earth. Souls can feel guilty for things they did while incarnate and they do have and show remorse to my clients when visiting. Soul groups and members have personalities too, sometimes joking with my client during the visit and other times being more serious.

All of us have characters in our lives who are challenging. We might have a sibling who we haven't gotten along with in decades, or a conditionally loving parent, or a physically abusive partner, or a competitive coworker who always tries to outdo us. Oftentimes these characters are members of your soul group who are incarnate with you for a reason. Regardless of how the character acts towards you on Earth, their higher self is very loving and understanding towards you in the soul realm. Soul group members are very candid with my clients; they answer questions directly and objectively.

It's helpful and reassuring to get awareness and clarity into the source or cause of some of the relationship issues we have with people incarnate with us. I find it has softened the rough edges a bit for me with some challenging people. What is helpful to understand about the higher self of humans on Earth is that their higher selves *know* when their incarnated selves are not doing well on their path or misbehaving or are not being kind. Our higher selves can only guide and make suggestions to our human selves; they cannot force us to do anything. Our free will has control.

A good example of this was Bernadette who was estranged from her father. Upon seeing her father's higher self in her soul group, the first comment Bernadette made was, "He seems nicer here." I asked why that was and Bernadette got the answer, "He doesn't have as much responsibility here" ("here" meant the soul realm). A few more questions helped us determine that her father chose responsibility to be the lesson he was to work on in his current incarnation, but he was not doing well with that lesson. Her father's soul had good intentions; however, it turned out to be more difficult than he anticipated. Consequently, he had been dumping much of his responsibility onto others in his life, and hence, the estrangement from many members of his family. Bernadette later admitted that learning this information helped her to have a better understanding of her father.

Another example is Darcy, who had belonged to a church with a large congregation. She was heavily involved with the church as a volunteer and did much work to help it be successful. Then she and the congregation learned the minister was having an affair with one of the church administrators while both were married to others. This situation tore the congregation apart. The minister left the church, half the congregation followed him, and Darcy was left with the other half to figure out how to rebuild their spiritual community. Fast forward a few years, and Darcy was now a lay minister of a non-denominational congregation elsewhere and was doing very well on her spiritual path. Then during her between life session with me when she is about to meet with her soul group members, guess who was the first soul to step forward: the soul who was *that* minister! Darcy immediately asked, "What is *HE* doing here?" She was not happy with seeing his soul in her group. Well, he was a member of her soul group even though he was the last person she would have ever imagined to be there. I asked the minister's soul why he did the deeds that ended up tearing the church's congregation apart. He responded, "It was necessary in order to set Darcy on her spiritual path for growth."

This is an excellent example of a soul group member *choosing* at the soul level before incarnation to play an unkind role in order to help another soul in their group work on their lesson.

Perspectives of Soul Group and Primary Soul Mate

The following drawing, Figure 1, is provided to give you an idea of what your soul group includes. The view of this scene is from the perspective of a client meeting with their group in the soul realm. When my client meets with their soul group, they are typically escorted there by their guide who is the soul guide for the entire group. The soul guide then stands next to my client or even slightly away from her while the members of the group take turns coming forward to converse with her.

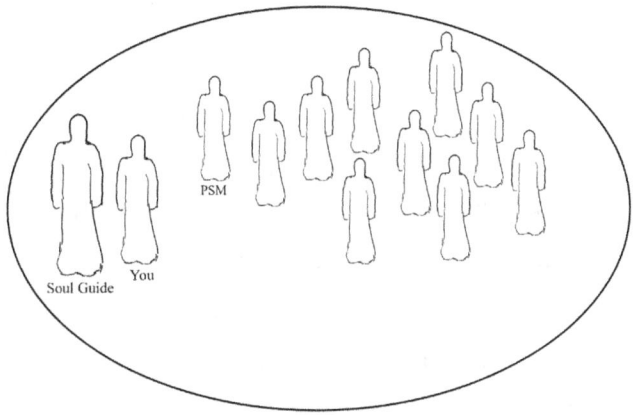

Figure 1. Your soul group.

Members of your group present themselves to you as their most recent incarnation so that you recognize them. When a client is having a session with me, they are experiencing every part of the session from their current human perspective, which includes the memory from their current life.

Now a key point to remember is that you will incarnate with your group over and over again; each of you take on different roles each time to help yourself and others work on their lessons. There is typically one member of the soul group who is known as the primary soul mate (PSM) and this soul is the one who incarnates most frequently with my client. The PSM is also the one soul group member who you tend to be the closest with in your various incarnations. Often times a PSM is your romantic partner but not always. Sometimes they are a best friend, a grandparent, or even an aunt in your current life.

I worked with a couple who have been married for over fifty years, and I conducted past life and between life sessions for both, separately of course. It turns out that they are not each other's PSMs. Hers is her best friend who died a few years earlier, his PSM is his grandson.

A good question brought up by a workshop attendee was, "Are soul group members always about the same age as they incarnate together?" For clarity, the question related to human years and the answer was "No." If your parents and possibly your grandparents are part of your soul group, then obviously, they have to incarnate decades before you. As you can see in the prior example of the couple who have been married for decades, the husband was born first and the soul of his grandson, his primary soul mate, waited six decades before he incarnated to take the role of his grandson. This example supports why one soul might wait six months in human time to rein-carnate but another soul in your group might wait fifty-plus years to come into their next role.

A related question is whether the members of a soul group are the same soul age. They are similar in age as most of them joined the group at about the same time when their souls were born and were assigned a soul guide to work with them. The souls in the group are about the same age but will certainly vary a bit regarding soul evolution based on the paths, lessons, and do-overs. As I explained about my own soul group, two members joined our group later and are a bit younger from a soul evolution perspective.

Exceptions to Having a Soul Group

Not all souls incarnate on Earth belong to a soul group. Others may have a soul group that is much smaller than described in this chapter. The exceptions are the Interplanetary souls. Remember the souls who have spent most of their incarnations elsewhere such as another planet, a star, or a different galaxy? Sometimes these Interplanetary souls come to Earth either alone or with a small number of souls who joined them on their journey.

To conclude, our soul groups are dear to us. We

have committed to work with our soul group members for a very long time as we work on our lessons in this Earth dimension. There is too much to learn here to go it alone, so we take on the lessons and then meet up again in the soul realm, just to do it all over again with our next incarnations.

Exercise

To consider the list of possible characters who might be in your soul group, list eight to ten significant people in your life, living or deceased. Then list the challenges, if any, you have or had with each person. The final part of this exercise is to think about each person, your challenges with them, and then contemplate which lesson each person might be helping you to work on. You will need additional paper for this exercise. Write up the following for each character you identify.

○ Name:

○ Relationship:

○ Challenge(s):

○ Lesson:

NOTES:

_____

_____

_____

_____

_____

_____

_____

_____

_____

_____

_____

_____

_____

_____

CHAPTER 10

Selecting Our Life Lessons

Before our soul incarnates into its next lifetime, we first must decide which lesson we are going to work on in that lifetime. Our souls do not make this decision alone; instead, it's a joint decision we make with our soul guide. Since our soul guides are very familiar with our soul's progress to date and have been through the experiences themselves, it's helpful and appreciated to have their advice to guide us in this decision.

Following is a short list of the life lessons our souls choose to work on in various lifetimes. Although the list is not complete, it will provide you with an idea of common lessons as we continue the discussion.

- ✿ ~ Self-love
- ✿ ~ Assertiveness
- ✿ ~ Standing up for yourself
- ✿ ~ Helping others
- ✿ ~ Compassion
- ✿ ~ Strength
- ✿ ~ Independence
- ✿ ~ Overcoming addictions
- ✿ ~ Forgiveness
- ✿ ~ Perseverance
- ✿ ~ Responsibility
- ✿ ~ Overcoming abandonment
- ✿ ~ Being an advocate for others
- ✿ ~ Overcoming discrimination

On Lesson Levels and How We Choose a Life Lesson

There is no formal list of life lessons that we each work on in a specific sequence. But some lessons are geared towards the new/beginner souls and others are intended for the more advanced souls who have had more experience on Earth.

For example, I consider learning self-love to be one of the foundational lessons needed before taking on more difficult lessons such as forgiveness and overcoming addiction.

Now you might be examining the above list and wondering, "Why would I agree to take on the lesson of forgiveness? That sounds challenging!" The thing to remember about your souls in the soul realm is that they are quite objective and willing because when in the soul realm, our souls are more interested in growth and evolving, and are not worried about the pain that will be endured during a lifetime. And a lifetime is temporary, a short time period compared to eternity in the soul realm. A ninety-year life on Earth seems like a long time to us humans, but it's a mere blip in time to the soul realm. Here is where the analogy of a stage play is useful to continue this conversation.

Imagine as a beginner actor you have just completed basic acting lessons and you are now ready to try on some acting roles. You have signed up to be represented by an agent (a similar role to your soul guide), and it's your agent's job to find roles for you and negotiate the terms. In the beginning, your access to roles will be limited because you have no formal experience yet, so you will take on some easy roles that help you become comfortable with acting and refine your abilities. The same can be said of your beginner roles on Earth as a newer soul. Some of the first roles may merely be giving your soul experience being in a physical body and learning to maneuver with Earth realm requirements: basic survival skills of finding food, shelter, and clothing, and then the more fundamental skills of learning to sustain yourself with work and navigating relationships with others. Your soul guide will work with your soul to determine which roles are most appropriate for your soul's level of development. The list of lessons your soul has already completed is key in determining which lessons your soul is ready to proceed with next. And your own soul has a strong hand in deciding which lessons you are ready for as well. Your soul guide might show you two or three lessons that your soul is ready for and you get to select the one you want.

As your soul gains experience in the Earth realm, your soul is then more prepared to take on the more difficult lessons. If a lesson requires the physical body or mental ability to be severely handicapped or challenged, the soul does not preview that life saying, "That looks too hard. I don't want to do that life." Instead, at the soul level, we know the role on Earth is temporary and only for a short duration.

The challenges associated with that lifetime are also temporary, but will provide an excellent opportunity for the soul to learn, grow, and evolve; therefore, it's worth it. This is very similar to an actor taking on a very challenging role that in turn will further develop their acting abilities.

A previous boss of mine used a phrase called "stretch assignments." These were the assignments that a particular employee had not taken on before, but with their prior experience and some additional guidance from management they could do the job. Such assignments enabled his staff to *stretch* their abilities. Our souls do the same; with help and guidance from our soul guides, we take on stretch assignments. I often think of Dustin Hoffman when he took the role of Raymond in the 1988 movie, *Rain Man*. He had never played a person with autism before, and this role is a good example of a stretch assignment that he signed up for. He took on extra work to learn how to play an adult man with autism in that movie, and he went on to win an Academy Award for it. I consider this to be a stretch assignment for him and he succeeded. Our souls do the same.

During a regression, I always ask my client's soul guide what lesson my client chose to work on in the past life we visited. I also ask a follow-up question, "Did my client complete that lesson?" If the answer is "No," then it certainly provides a topic of contemplation for the client regarding their current life.

Upon Returning to the Soul Realm

When a soul returns to the soul realm after completing a lifetime on Earth, they are always greeted by their soul guide and lovingly accepted back into the soul realm.

After that soul has reacclimated to the frequency/vibration of the soul realm and become reacquainted with their soul guide, normally the two of them will spend some time together reviewing the life that was just completed.

What's very interesting and unique about this review is that the soul who just completed the lifetime is now very objective in the review of that life. When a soul completes a life on Earth and leaves the physical body, they also leave the residue of the ego and pride with the physical body and these traits do not follow the soul to the soul realm. It is for this reason that our souls can objectively review the lifetime and clearly state, "Yes, I can see where I was working on the lesson rather well for a while but then I got a taste of blaming others for my problems and chose to continue on that path and turned away from the work I needed to do. And I will need to continue working on that lesson in the next lifetime."

Learning Also Occurs in the Soul Realm

Earth is not the only place where we learn. We also learn in the soul realm between lifetimes, and the things we learn there are aimed at helping our souls grow and evolve and to also help us prepare for our future lessons on Earth.

When I started learning about the soul realm and the teachings that occur there, I wondered why our souls just couldn't learn everything there and skip the Earth part? Through additional study I learned why: There are things we learn on Earth that cannot be taught in the soul realm because there is only loving energy in the soul realm. For instance, we cannot learn the lesson of forgiveness in the soul realm because nothing happens there to necessitate forgiveness. In contrast, there are plenty of opportunities on Earth to help our souls engage in this lesson. Souls do not steal from, betray, hurt, or kill each other in the soul realm, but humans certainly do that to each other on Earth.

When we prepare for an incarnation and we have selected the specific lesson to work on, we then get to choose the body, region, family, and culture we are going to be born into. This will be discussed in much more detail in the next chapter, Scripting Our Lives

Exercise

Take a look at this brief list of life lessons and see if one or two resonate with you. Think of the challenges you have had in your life that may make one or two lessons on this list stand out for you. You can even add lessons to this list.

- Self-love
- Assertiveness
- Standing up for yourself
- Helping others
- Compassion
- Strength
- Independence
- Overcoming addiction
- Forgiveness
- Perseverance
- Responsibility
- Overcoming abandonment
- Being an advocate for others
- Overcoming discrimination

NOTES:

_____

_____

_____

_____

_____

_____

_____

_____

_____

_____

_____

_____

_____

_____

_____

CHAPTER 11

Scripting Our Lives

Once we have worked with our soul guide to select the particular life lesson we intend to focus on during our upcoming incarnation, we now need to *script* the main components of that life before we are born into it. You are probably wondering if you read that correctly. Yes, you script the main components of your life!

For example, in the soul realm let's say you select "overcoming abandonment" as the main lesson to work on in your upcoming life. Your soul guide will then show you three to four options to support that lesson. Each option includes the type of physical body (male, female, race/ethnicity, body build, healthy or not, and so on), the region of the world where you incarnate, the type of family environment you will be born into (culture, loving or not, religious beliefs, number of siblings, etc.), and you even select your sexual orientation. As you script your life, you choose who your parents are going to be, your significant other(s), children, siblings, and more.

Our soul group members all work together in the soul realm to decide who's going to play each role. Next, you need conditions in that life that will provide your soul with the opportunity to work on that lesson; therefore, you choose the circumstances, events, and even the challenges you will face. With the lesson of overcoming abandonment, you might choose, for example, to be given up for adoption at birth, deserted by your father at a young age, being gay and born into an extremely conservative family who ostracizes you, or possibly lose both parents in an accident while you are a child.

Our Souls Are Objective

When we are in the soul realm working out the details of our next life, our souls are completely objective. Think for a moment that as a human you are tasked with writing a stage play titled "Fran Overcomes Abandonment." For this play, the first scene is Fran's birth and the final scene is Fran's death. All the scenes in between are aimed at supporting Fran's quest to overcome being abandoned in that life. As the writer for this two-hour production, you cannot script every single thought or action that will take place in Fran's daily life of eighty years; instead, you script the main components.

As the writer of this play, you are *objective* and you do not get hung up on the emotional aspects of Fran's challenges. You do not skip writing an intense abandonment scene because you don't want Fran's character to encounter emotional pain. Instead, you include that painful scene because it's part of the overall play to show how Fran learns to overcome abandonment.

This stage play scenario is very similar to how our souls write or script our lives for upcoming lessons. Our souls do not get mired in the potential emotional aspects of the upcoming lifetime because at the soul level and while working in the soul realm, we see the life as a very short stint in the overall evolution of our eternal soul.

An eighty-year life on Earth becomes a "speck" of time in the big picture of our eternal being. Regardless of the challenges faced in a human lifetime, when the soul returns to the soul realm after a life is completed, it will be whole and perfect.

As our souls advance, the lessons we take on become more difficult and we often take on those stretch assignments mentioned in the last chapter. Oftentimes *one lesson* requires multiple lifetimes to complete it. Some of us have been incarnated hundreds or even thousands of times in this Earthly dimension.

The topic of scripting our lives can be rather difficult to accept, especially if you had a very difficult life fraught with abuse, abandonment, health issues, or losses. You wonder "Why would I *CHOOSE* to have these challenges in my life?" But there is a reason for every one of them. We may not know the reason or the purpose of these difficulties right now, but the sole reason overall is for our soul to learn.

Free Will

The learning can be challenging and that's where free will comes in. Although our souls choose our lessons and script our lives, something unique happens once we are born: we gain the attribute of *free will*. With free will, we can choose to face our challenges and do something positive about them or we can choose to *not* face our challenges, blaming others for our problems and/or becoming complete victims to our circumstances, or perhaps both.

There are times when we just want to run away from our challenges and not deal with them. Leaving an abusive relationship, acknowledging an addiction, or even learning to stand up for ourselves can sometimes seem like insurmountable tasks, especially if we have let them go on for decades. But if we walk away from our challenges, our beautiful, loving soul guide will be right there to provide us with more opportunities to face our challenges over and over again in a given lifetime. I like to use the following diagram in Figure 2 to emphasize my point. The first scenario is our birth, life, and death on a straight line, which means we did everything perfectly: the right choices, never hurting anyone, and completing every challenge perfectly as it was presented during our lifetime:

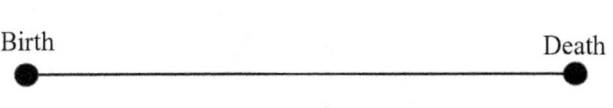

(Not common)

Figure 2. The "perfect life."

This drawing is not a realistic depiction of most incarnations: we rarely experience a straight line from birth to the end of life. The exception to this scenario, however, are children and babies who pass away. These beautiful souls come into their Earth incarnation for a short time to do their work and then leave. This emotional and challenging topic is discussed further in the next chapter.

Do any of us truly complete our life without any hiccups along the way? Most likely the answer is "no." Besides, where would the learning happen in such a scenario? Figure 3 shows a more realistic representation, meaning that we weave on and off our path throughout life, experiencing the ups and downs as we are confronted with our scripted challenges, and learning along the way. Free will allows for such weaving about and this is normal.

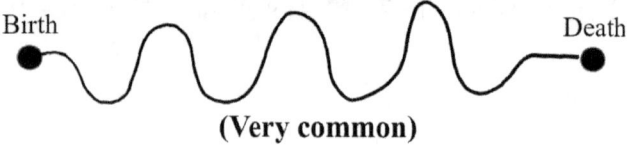

(Very common)

Figure 3. The "realistic life."

We have free will all along the way but how do we know when we are going off our path? How do we know when we have made a decision whether it's the right one? This is a good time to bring up the option of following our *gut feelings*. Whether you want to call it your "intuition," your "gut," or just a *feeling*, these are the signs our guides, our higher self, and even the universe provides to help you know if you are on the right path.

At some point you probably had a feeling in the pit of your stomach that guided you to or steered you away from a situation. I have often felt that if you follow your gut feelings, then you will probably stay rather close to your predestined path. But sometimes there are temptations, right? Sometimes temptations just seem to be more fun! Several years ago, I participated in a five-day cattle drive and I enjoyed some interesting conversations around the campfire in the evenings. One such conversation was about gut feelings and someone provided their definition of gut: "God's urgent tug."

When we venture off our path we are provided many opportunities to get back on it. When you get that gut feeling about a situation but choose not to follow it, that's a clue that you are venturing off your path. When we get off track and mess up, our loving guides give us many, many, many opportunities to return to our path.

Do-overs

What happens if you don't adequately complete the lesson you chose to work on during a lifetime? You get what I call a "do-over" the next time around. Earlier in this chapter, I mentioned that it may take two or more lifetimes to complete a particular lesson. One thing I want to make very clear is that when our soul has to set up a lesson do-over, it is *NOT* retribution or punishment for failing to complete the lesson in the previous incarnation. We are simply provided another opportunity to work on the lesson. And our soul will orchestrate opportunities over and over again until we complete it.

I will use the analogy of a grandfather teaching his four-year-old grandson to tie his shoes to explain how our guides help us. After showing his grandson the many steps involved with tying shoes, the grand-father lets the child try it on his own. He watches patiently as the little boy tightens the laces and makes one loop, but that's where the child starts to struggle and cannot finish the task. The grandfather puts a loving arm around the boy's shoulders, praises him on his successful steps and then gently guides his grandson on the remaining steps. Each time the boy ties his shoe, he accomplishes a little more than the previous attempt until he finally gets his shoe tied. Our soul guides do the same for us. After a lifetime where our soul did not complete the lesson, our benevolent guide will stand next to us, review with us what went well and what did not, and then help us prepare for the next time around, the do-over. No negative judgment, punishment, or penalty. Most often our soul will get additional training in the soul realm in areas that help us to be more successful in the next incarnation with the lesson.

What's interesting about a do-over is that the circumstances and characters for the lesson in the next lifetime will change, but the lesson is the same. We might as well deal with the lesson this time and finish it so that we can move on to the next one!

Balancing

No matter what sex you were born into in your current life, I can say with much confidence that you have been a different sex in other lives. We have all had lives as female, male, poor, rich, healthy, sickly, kind, and mean. If you have had a life where you oppressed other humans, such as a slave trader, it's quite possible that in a subsequent lifetime you will be enslaved or otherwise oppressed. This is by no means justice or punishment for what you did in the prior lifetime. It's actually a *balancing* of your experience. You might have endured a lifetime of grinding poverty but the next lifetime was filled with material abundance. It's basically your soul's learning to experience both sides of an experience (and everything in between).

In my first session with Barbara, she visited a past life that seemed very similar to her current life: a woman, financially well off, very happy, and comfortable. But in the second past life regression Barbara had, she visited a lifetime as a young man who was married and had one young child. Sadly, in that lifetime the man lived in poverty and was stressed as he struggled daily to put food on the table. When I asked Barbara's soul guide why that particular life was shown to her, he responded, "To show her she has experienced both types of lifetimes, one with financial struggle and one without." This is another example of how a soul experiences both sides of a situation in order to understand the feelings, complexities, benefits, and challenges associated with both sides. The soul then has a balanced experienced.

There are many examples of client sessions where it was clear that their choice to incarnate as gay or lesbian was a pre-birth choice. One such example is Niel, whom I met at a talk he gave at a spiritual center I frequent. Niel is a gay man in his sixties who has been with his partner for over twenty years. During Niel's talk, he said, "At the soul level, I chose to be gay in this incarnation. Once I was *conceived*, I no longer had a choice. I am gay and that's how this lifetime will be."

Victimhood

The free will choice of being a victim to your life circumstances is not an appropriate way to spend your life on Earth. You have probably come across a few people in your life who chose to be victims in their life. These are the people who prefer to blame every negative circumstance of their life on someone or something else, as if they are powerless to change any of it.

Quite frankly, there are going to be people who choose the victim route instead of working on their lessons. I will refrain from being harsh here because I have likely chosen to be a victim at some point or another in this life and in others. But eventually these souls do have to work on their lesson, their *stuff*. If not, they will get do-overs and their additional learning as they eventually accomplish the lesson and move on to the next one.

Suicide

Suicide, in most cases, is a free will choice and is the ultimate example of giving up on one's lesson. I say "in most cases" because I have come across a couple of clients who learned that the loved one they lost to suicide actually made a pre-birth decision to take their life to benefit another soul (to launch another soul onto a different life trajectory).

Free-will suicide undoubtedly requires a do-over for the souls who left their lesson incomplete.

Sometimes suicide is a recurrent pattern on a person's soul path. If I encounter a client who admits to having had thoughts of suicide at various times in their life, it doesn't surprise me when their past life regression entails visiting a life where they took their life. And there are times where the client doesn't admit to thoughts of suicide in their current life until after visiting a past life where they see they actually *did* take their life. This awareness allows me to elaborate on the topic of suicide with these clients.

Following are a few points I would like to share about suicide from a regression therapist's perspective:

As souls, we choose our life lesson/purpose, challenges, opportunities, and main events for each life before we enter it. We also chart in the approximate time of death, which basically occurs when we have completed what we came to do during a specific lifetime.

Suicide is usually *NOT* one of the pre-charted ways we choose to end our lives. Suicide is seen as a way of opting out of working on our life lesson/purpose.

✿

Suicide is a free-will choice for most, not a predestined path.

✿

By choosing suicide, the challenges left incomplete in that life will still need to be met in a future life; there is no escaping the lesson we signed up for, that is, the need to complete it.

✿

There is no penalty or retribution in the soul realm for those who choose suicide. But souls *ARE* shown the effects of the suicide on their surviving loved ones who have to live on without them.

✿

Suicide is sometimes a recurrent theme for souls and for this reason it is extremely important for these souls to *break the cycle*! People who are quick to consider suicide starting at a young age have probably done it before in previous lives, which is precisely why it is so important to not go through with it in order to break the cycle.

✿

People who take their life plant the idea of suicide into the minds of their survivors, especially the children. Sadly, I am aware of a few cases where a child lost a parent to suicide and took their own life later on.

If you have ever contemplated suicide, I plead with you to not do it. You matter so much! You are never a burden. You are a beautiful soul who has a purpose here and we need you! You will never be faced with challenges that your soul is not prepared to take on. Ask for help. That might very well be the lesson you chose to work on—*asking for help*. There are many resources to help people with suicidal thoughts; please refer to the Appendix for a list.

Scripted Suicide

Although it happens infrequently, there are times when suicide is *scripted* into a soul's life plan. Two examples follow.

Alani was an acquaintance of mine when she came to me for a regression. I had always known her to be reserved and pleasant but I didn't know much about her.

As we started her session, Alani provided me with some important history: Five years earlier she and her husband, Soren, had a terrible argument one evening and it ended when he slapped her. Extremely angry and hurt, Alani immediately left the room.

Moments later Soren found Alani and attempted to talk with her but she turned her back to him and told him to go away. Soren then went to another part of the house and shot himself.

Needless to say, Alani has journeyed a long road to recover from this tragedy and she still had some distance to go. Two months after Soren's death, she moved three thousand miles away to start a new life in Hawaii.

During her session with me, the following transpired when her soul guide joined us:

Shelly: What was the purpose
of Soren taking his life?

Guide: It was all about the love.

Shelly: Is Soren's soul available
to come for a visit?

Guide: Yes. (Alani then felt
Soren's soul embracing her.)

Shelly: What message does
Soren's soul have for Alani?

Soren's soul: I always loved
you and I always will.

Shelly: Why did you choose to die/
transition the way you did?

Soren's soul: Because I was tired and
stuck, and I knew it would catapult
Alani to a whole new world.

Shelly: What was the source of
your feeling tired and stuck?

Soren's soul: Isolation, fear, loneliness.

Shelly: Was your suicide free will or pre-planned before incarnating?

Soren's soul: Pre-planned.

Shelly: Do you have a message for Alani?

Soren's soul: Live largely, expand your spirit, be happy, and shine your light!

Obviously, this was a very emotional session. Since moving to Hawaii, Alani had learned reiki (a form of energy healing for the body) and was using this gift to help other people heal. And after some time processing this session, she realized that her life trajectory did change in a completely different direction as a result of Soren's passing, a trajectory that she now embraces.

When I had my own between-life session, my facilitator asked my high council if my brother's soul learned his lesson about suicide in the life he just ended. Their answer was, "No. He will have to lose a loved one to suicide in a future life for his soul to get the full lesson." In this case, someone in our soul group will *agree* to end their life in an upcoming incarnation (actually to script it into their life plan) so that my brother's soul will experience the loss from a different perspective and, hopefully, learn the lesson. It's not punishment, it's a balancing of the experience.

As we learn more about our souls and their evolvement, I ask that you refrain from judgment of others regarding their soul path, life choices, and level of evolvement. It's quite possible that the homeless woman you see on the street corner asking for money or the bad-boy brother of yours who cannot seem to stay away from drugs and jail time just might be advanced souls.

In *Bringing Your Soul to Light*, Linda Backman writes about the example of a client's grown daughter who is drug-addicted and homeless, yet the daughter's soul is advanced. The advanced soul of the daughter chose her difficult life path before incarnating to "try on a non-pristine life"; "her high level of soul development allows her to manage such a complex life."[1]

Do We Mess Up?

With a smile I say, "Of course we do!" None of us follows our respective path perfectly. Weaving on and

---

1 Dr. Linda Backman, *Bringing Your Soul to Light: Healing through Past Lives and the Time Between* (Llewellyn Publications, 2009).

off our path provides us with a multitude of opportunities to grow and learn from our mistakes. When we do veer away from our path we are provided with many opportunities to return to our path.

If your chosen lesson was to learn to stand up for yourself, then think of the many characters who keep coming into your life who give you an opportunity to practice exactly that: standing up for yourself. The lesson might take form in your workplace, with some of your family members, the friends you choose, or even the partners you take. The opportunities to learn *how* to stand up for yourself may come to you in a multitude of ways: a book that a friend offers to loan you, the invitation to join an online workshop that happens to appear in your email inbox, the guest speaker at your spiritual center on Sunday, or even the TED Talk title that catches your eye on Facebook.

It's perfectly acceptable to mess up on our path. Our guides have worked through these lessons and know very well how difficult and challenging the Earth lessons are; therefore, they do not judge us when we mess up. Instead, they provide us with more opportunities to work on our lessons and help us get back on our path when we veer off.

We veer off our paths often. We get many opportunities to get back on our path. Those who choose victimhood over working on their lesson will get more opportunities to come back and do it again; once more, it's okay when we mess up. Our guides never judge us for messing up. They love us unconditionally as they have been through Earth school themselves and know the challenges. They always provide guidance to help us move forward.

Exercise

Think back on your life and identify a time when you were at a crossroads and had to make a decision. What was that crossroad? Here are some hypothetical examples:

☼ Do I stay in this marriage or leave it?

☼ Do I go to the East Coast to go to college like I have planned for many years or do I stay home because this new girl I met a month ago seems like *the one* and I fear leaving her now?

☼ Do I leave this great-paying job that I hate?

☼ Do I run away because my father is abusing me or do I stay because if I leave he'll abuse my mother?

☼ What was a major dilemma in your life and what were the choices you had at the time?

☼ Did you follow your gut feeling when you made the choice?

✿ What positive things came from your choice?

✿ What negative effects resulted
from your decision?

✿ And the most important question:
What did you learn about yourself
through that experience?

CHAPTER 12

Life Challenges Are Opportunities

As a soul working with our soul guide to determine the components of our next life, why would we choose a challenging life or choose to have *ANY* challenges in our lives? Why not plan splendid, happy, prosperous lives full of fun, excitement, financial stability, and all without the challenges?

To answer these questions, let me ask you this: When do you feel you learned the most during your life thus far? When life was easy or when you encountered challenges? During my speaking engagements, attendees always nod their heads in agreement when

I mention "encountered challenges." As humans we learn, grow, and develop by working through our difficulties, challenges, mistakes, and losses. All of us have had many lives—difficult lives, easier lives, and all for a reason. But we must have challenging times in order to learn.

In this chapter I use the words "challenge" and "opportunity" interchangeably because they really are the same thing in this context. For example, if your soul chooses the *challenge* of being born to verbally abusive parents, you also have the *opportunity* to learn how to overcome being born to and raised by verbally abusive parents.

Our souls do not choose a life lesson that our soul is not capable of handling. For example, a young soul will not be guided to take on a challenge that is beyond the level of that soul.

Referring back to the K-12 example introduced in Chapter 4, we don't give our second-graders classes in trigonometry because that is higher level math reserved for high school when students are more prepared to handle it. In a similar context, younger souls will not take on more difficult lessons such as *forgiveness* until they are evolved to a point where they are ready.

Life Lessons and Corresponding Challenges

Let's imagine the scenario where your soul is with your soul guide in the soul realm and the two of you have agreed on the lesson you will take on for your next Earth incarnation.

This time I will use the example of *forgiveness* as the selected lesson. Now in order to learn and work on that lesson, you will need opportunities in the upcoming lifetime that will provide you with the chance to work on forgiveness. If you return to the scenario of writing a stage play and this time it is titled, "Fran Learns Forgiveness," what scenes would you create in that stage play to tell the story? Even looking at your own life right now, what challenges throughout your current life have provided you with opportunities to work on forgiving others? Or, more importantly, forgiving yourself? Following is an example of a client who learned she is working on forgiveness.

Personal Story

Sofia was fifty-two years old, married thirty years, and had five children. When her youngest child, a daughter named Amber, was ten years old she was sexually molested by her uncle, Sofia's brother. Amber forgave her uncle and then tragically died in a car accident three years later. Sofia has been unable to forgive her brother for what he did to her daughter and she still struggles with the loss of her child.

I regressed Sofia to a past life and she enters a scene as a seventeen-year-old girl who had just been raped. She feels emotionally heavy in that scene, has physical pain, and is trying to walk home. As we progress through scenes in that life, she gives birth to a boy as a result of the rape, and she and her family love the child and raise him together. During that lifetime she never forgave the man who raped her.

After that past life ends and Sofia's soul has returned to the soul realm, her soul guide, Clyde, joins her and I proceed to ask Clyde questions on Sofia's behalf (only highlights are included):

Shelly: What lesson was Sofia's soul to learn in that past life?

Clyde: Forgiveness.

Shelly: Did her soul complete the lesson of forgiveness?

Clyde: Definitely not.

Shelly: Did Sofia's soul bring any unresolved karma from that life to her current life?

Clyde: Yes, with her daughter, and it came forth as the sexual abuse her daughter endured from Sofia's brother in her current life. Her lesson this time is to forgive her brother.

This regression is a straightforward example of how a soul did not complete a lesson in a past life and, therefore, arranged a do-over. Again, it's not a punishment for not finishing the lesson, but rather another opportunity to complete the lesson. Although the lesson of forgiveness is the same, the circumstances and characters changed. All three souls—Sofia, her brother, and her daughter—agreed to the roles and circumstances before incarnating in this life.

The most important result of this session is that Sofia realized the need to work diligently on learning forgiveness in this lifetime so that another do-over becomes unnecessary. It's important to note that to forgive cannot be a flippant "Fine, I forgive him!" and walk away. It must be an authentic, deep from the heart and soul forgiveness. We cannot fool our guides and higher self—they always know when we are truthful and not.

Lesson and Challenge of Losing a Child

Nothing is more personally devastating than losing a child. I have met so many people who have lost children to drowning, car accidents, overdoses, and suicide, and all of them are tragedies. Some marriages survived these tragedies and others did not. The strain of loss, guilt, shame, and one partner moving forward in life and the other one stuck in misery, can take a toll on us personally and in our relationships.

It has been my experience that many children who die young are actually advanced souls who *agreed* to incarnate for a short time in order to help someone else work on a life lesson. For example: a baby born prematurely, who struggles to survive, then dies six months later in the hospital may have purposely chosen this path in order to help one or both of his parents work on their lesson of compassion. The child born with extreme cerebral palsy and needs constant care might have chosen this life to help her family members learn patience or unconditional love.

In the prior example of Sofia losing her thirteen-year-old daughter in a car accident, her daughter's soul *chose* her role and short life in order to help her mother work on forgiveness. These children who pass away leave early because they accomplished what they intended to do in their lives and then it was time to return home to the soul realm. Some of my clients have received messages from children who have passed, as in the following example.

Personal Story

Nora found me through a friend who recently had a session with me. When I first spoke with Nora on the phone she asked good questions about how a session worked but she seemed a bit reserved. I sensed some hesitation on her part, and really didn't know whether she was ready for a session. She came to my office a few days later and as we were going through the questionnaire, I learned why she was a bit reserved; she told me her adult son, Shane, died four years earlier from taking a drug he bought off the Internet that was tainted with something deadly. He had recently moved in with his parents, and Nora was the one who found his body. She was obviously heartbroken and she was wondering if a regression would shed any light on why she manifested this awful loss in her life.

Nora's regression was going well and we reached a point in her session where her soul guide, Cassiopeia, had joined us. After asking many other questions about her life, I then posed the following questions about Shane's passing.

Shelly: Was Shane's death pre-planned at the soul level (before birth) or was it free will?

Cassiopeia: Pre-planned.

Shelly: What was the purpose of Shane's death in Nora's life?

Cassiopeia: Nora thought Shane was hers and even Shane thought he was hers, but he is a child of the universe. She didn't get to own him. While Nora loved Shane and was proud of him, he had his own soul and his own mission. He taught Nora to never take anything for granted and to show all the love she can, and to be forgiving and to be herself, to love deeper and more compassionately. Although Shane's death causes Nora to seek solitude, she actually relishes and looks for the very best in other people when she is with them. And she easily forgives others. Shane is always around her, he wants her to live her life, and his death has brought his parents closer together than they have ever been before. He wants them to enjoy their years together, he wants her to smile and know it's not her fault. He is sorry.

At this point, Nora told me her son almost died two times while growing up. I saw this as an example of exit points that I learned about in a book by Sylvia Browne. (I describe exit points at the end of Nora's story.)

Shelly: Is Shane's soul available to come for a visit?

Cassiopeia: Yes.

(Note: Nora is still hypnotized, relaxed in the recliner, eyes closed, and visiting with her soul guide in the soul realm.)

Nora then sees Shane's soul and says, "He looks so fresh, he looks taller, and he's so handsome, he has a wonderful wide smile. He's happy to see me and he puts his arms around me, we hug." Shane's soul proceeds to say many things to Nora and she is quite emotional at this time. "Mom, I know you love me but you have to think about other things, you can't just think about me all the time. I'm going to be with you soon enough, I watch over all of you, I am always with you. Just feel my presence and know that I love you and you were a great mom."

Next, I asked Shane's soul a couple of questions:

Shelly: Shane, do you have a specific sign for *Nora* to know when your soul is around her?

Shane: I can transfer my consciousness to a couple of beings: deer and large birds of prey (hawks, eagles, and osprey). I also appear as the cardinals she sees daily in her yard.

Shelly: Shane, are you an Interplanetary soul or an Earth soul?

Shane: Interplanetary. I came with my mom's soul to Earth, we are from the same place, we are soul mates in the same soul group.

I know reading this section does not remove the pain and struggle from losing a child, but sometimes it softens the rough edges a bit.

I do not promote my regression business as a means of getting in touch with deceased loved ones.

That is not the intent of past life regression work and is best left to those skilled in mediumship. However, there are times when I feel that I am guided during a client session to ask if the soul of the deceased is available to come visit my client. I will do this when my client is truly struggling with moving forward from the loss.

There have been some occasions where my client's soul guide says the soul of the loved one is not available for a visit; thus, there is no guarantee. With my clients who have lost children, I ask their guides, "What was the purpose of my client losing their child?" We always get the answer.

The exit points mentioned above were introduced to me when I read a book by Sylvia Browne, a known psychic and medium who has written over twenty books. I have read much of her work and I apologize for not recalling the specific title of the book in which she discussed exit points. The gist of the concept is that as a soul we script into our upcoming lifetime three or more exit points where that life may come to an end.

We use only one of those exit points, that is, when our soul has finished the work it set out to do in that lifetime.

Relationship Challenges

There are a variety of reasons why people come into a relationship, whether as a couple, siblings, parent and child, best friends, boss and employee, co-workers, and so on. The overall reason is learning. We get into relationships with others to help one another work on our lessons. Your soul always takes on the role of teacher by providing other humans the chance to work on their lessons by interacting with you. In turn, they act as a teacher for you by providing many chances to learn from them.

Before incarnating, your soul makes an agreement, sometimes called a "soul contract," whereupon you each agree to the lesson and to the challenges that you present one another as a means of learning and working on your chosen lesson. For example, your soul may agree to take on the role of husband to another soul who agrees to be your wife. The soul who will be your wife has chosen a lesson of *overcoming addiction* while your soul is going to work on *patience*. At the pre-birth stage of planning, the two of you also agree that if her free will allows her to face her addiction and overcome it, then you will stay together as a couple. But if her free will keeps her in denial and she does not overcome it, then you will take your children and leave her. You will then continue your lesson of patience by dealing with her as an ex-wife with addiction issues and you will raise your children with little help from her. This is a hypothetical situation to make my point, but it could very well be a real-life scenario.

Personal Story

Following is an interesting relationship story from my client Valerie. Valerie and her husband Chris had been married for seven years and they had two young children, ages three and five years. During the beginning of the session where we discussed Valerie's life and circumstances, she admitted she wasn't sure about staying in her marriage. Chris was a good man and there was no abuse, she just didn't feel committed to him. Although much more was covered in her session, henceforth I focus on the relationship part for this example.

Valerie visited a past life in the 1900s as a very pregnant, twenty-year-old woman. She was not married and the father of her unborn baby was sent off to fight in WWII. Her pregnancy caused her family and community to shun her. At this time during the regression, she has just learned of her lover's death.

She is standing at the edge of the ocean and she jumps in and starts to sink; she does not want to live without her beloved. A man pulls her from the water, takes her to his home and nurses her back to health. Not long afterwards, he delivers her baby and the two of them end up staying together as a couple. He took her in when no one else would. Although her new partner is loving and provides a comfortable, simple home for her and her child, she never fully commits her love to him because her heart is still attached to her "true" love lost in the war. We reached a point in the session where her soul guide, Gareth, is present, and I asked the following questions on her behalf.

> *Shelly*: What was Valerie's soul to learn in that past life?

> *Gareth*: In that life she was to learn to let go of the people she lost. She was to learn to move forward, how to honor her path. But she never did.

> *Shelly*: Did Valerie's soul bring any unresolved karma from that past life to her current life?

> Gareth: Yes, she is holding on too firmly to things that aren't hers.

Shelly: What can Valerie do to resolve this?

Gareth: Let go and appreciate this life, appreciate who's here now. Chris loves her and she needs to love him back. She is doing it again in this life. There isn't a better match for her than Chris, [she needs to] appreciate him. The man she lost in that past life is the same soul as Sean (Valerie's ex-boyfriend) in this life. Her past love in that life was taken.

Shelly: Was that scenario in the past life part of their pre-birth plan between their two souls?

Gareth: Yes, he had to be taken in order for her to have a dramatic shift in that life.

I asked Valerie if all of this made sense to her, and she said that it did. Valerie admitted she hadn't been letting her husband *in*, that she had been resisting his love. Two months later we met for coffee to discuss how she was doing.

Valerie admitted the session allowed her to remove the block she had of accepting her husband's love and she saw a dramatic shift in their relationship for the better. She now realizes he is the best husband she can possibly have in this life and she looks at their relationship from a completely different, positive perspective. Beautiful!

Alternative Lifestyle Challenges

There are souls who choose an alternative lifestyle, such as being gay or lesbian, in order to learn and accept how others will treat them, or to learn to stand up for themselves, especially if they are born into a non-accepting family. Here is an example from Rachel's session. Rachel has a son who is gay and she wondered why his soul chose this. Rachel's only concern with her son's alternative life choice was about the challenges he'll face in his lifetime from those who are not accepting of him. During her session I asked her soul guide that exact question.

Shelly: Why did Rachel's son choose to be gay in his current life?

Thomas: To experience discrimination.

Shelly: What can Rachel do to help him on his path?

Thomas: Be patient.

Physical Challenges, Somatic Issues

When we have physical problems, we usually visit a physician or other health care provider to get treatment. Whether it is temporary help for a bacterial infection or a longer-term issue such as cancer, seeking treatment is the right thing to do. Part of the discussion at the beginning of a client session is for me to learn about the physical issues a client has had or is still having to deal with.

The reason this is important is because I will ask my client's soul guide what purpose those issues have in my client's life as well as the source of the issues, and specifically whether the source is in a past life.

I have noticed a trend in the death scenes in clients' past lives. If a client encountered a sudden or traumatic death, then oftentimes their soul brings forth remnants of that physical death into their current life in the form of somatic issues. Their soul memory brings things forward. Coming up next is an example of a client who has asthma.

I met Seanté when we were in college and worked at a department store together; soon after meeting we became roommates. She had asthma throughout her life and an inhaler was standard equipment she kept in her purse. The following is what we discovered during her past life regression.

Personal Story

Seanté enters a scene standing on the shore, overlooking an expanse of water and there is a green dome over the scene. It is not on Earth or another planet, but rather a star. Seanté's soul is Interplanetary and she is visiting a past life on a star in a physical body that is not human. The next few scenes Seanté describes are of her gliding underwater through caverns and tunnels.

Her body is the shape and color of a small beluga whale and her eyes look similar to that of a seal. As she glides through the water she senses she is being propelled by her tail, not fins or arms. She is completely alone on this planet and comfortable with her surroundings and we learn from her soul guide that she volunteered to stay on that planet until its existence ended. All the other beings like her had left the star but she was to stay to ensure all was well until the end. Her soul volunteered for this assignment. When I took her to her last day in that life, she was back on that shoreline where she was in the first scene, but this time a few things were different. The angle was tilted because she was not standing up, instead, she was laying on her side and looking at the water and horizon. The horizon is no longer a beautiful blue/green, it is now purplish red from gases. The water is dark and choppy. Her eyes gently close as her life and the life of the star end.

Seanté's soul guide, Flutter, joins us and I proceed to ask questions. Here is Flutter's response regarding Seanté's health:

Shelly: What is the source of asthma in Seanté's current life?

Flutter: The gas from the prior life, difficulty breathing this [Earth] air.

Shelly: What can she do to resolve/reduce this?

Flutter: She's doing it, breathing techniques, she is still learning it.

Shelly: What is the source of arthritis in her current body?

Flutter: Wear and tear of this planet [Earth] abused the body, [she has been] careless about certain things with her body.

Shelly: What can she do to help resolve/remove this?

Flutter: Water, swimming.

Most often, visiting the source of a somatic issue in a past life resolves the issue in the current life. As for Seanté, she had already been working on her asthma for fifteen-plus years and had made much progress on her own to reduce its occurrence.

Wake-up Calls

Challenging health conditions sometimes happen as a wake-up call to get our lives back on track when we have either gotten way off track or are on our way towards doing so. This is not your soul guide punishing you or the universe getting back at you for mistakes you have made. These are conditions you and your soul guide determined at pre-birth that may happen if you need a wake-up call. Your soul guide and your higher self are always trying to guide your human self towards your selected path but we, as humans, often don't listen. Following are a few examples from my clients.

Peter had a tumor in one ear when he was in his fifties. He had surgery to rid himself of the tumor;

he is now cancer free but he completely lost hearing in that ear. I asked his soul guide, "What was the purpose of Peter getting cancer and losing his hearing in one ear?" The reply was, "He needed to lose his hearing because he wasn't listening. He wasn't listening to Spirit." I then asked Peter's soul guide if he's listening now or has more work to do? "He has resolved it but the more he gets in touch with Spirit the happier he's going to be." At the conclusion of Peter's session, I asked him if losing half of his hearing changed his life. He said, "Most definitely. It got me back on my spiritual path."

Kerra was in her late twenties and had been diagnosed with lupus two years earlier. During her session I asked her soul guide, "What was the purpose of Kerra having lupus in her life?" Her guide's response, "To slow her down, she was going too fast, this [lupus] makes her listen." Afterward I asked Kerra if she knew what her guide's response meant. She said that she did know, and explained to me her life was heading very quickly down a path she *thought* she wanted: marriage, children, a house with the picket fence, but all with the wrong man. When the relationship abruptly ended, Kerra did not go through the proper healthy channels to recover and she drove her body into awakening the lupus inside her. After a long struggle to regain her health, Kerra has learned to slow down, listen to her body and, equally important, listen to her guide and higher self for guidance in her daily life. She later met and married her perfect partner, and they now have a beautiful daughter together. Kerra is grateful for what having lupus has taught her.

Abandonment

Overcoming abandonment is another big lesson. I speak of this from the perspective of adopted children who, most often, are adopted and raised by loving families, yet they still grow up with abandonment stigma: "My birth mother didn't love me enough to keep me." One of my own family members has two adopted children from his previous marriage. One of his children went into a rehab program at the age of twenty-one and *half* of the young adults in that program were adopted. Many of them have abandonment issues that lead to poor self-esteem and sometimes drug and alcohol abuse. This is a difficult lesson. Of course, not all adopted children have difficulties—many move forward with their lesson and master overcoming abandonment.

Catastrophic Events

What is the purpose of catastrophic events where large numbers of people are lost? For example, 6 million Jewish people perished in the Holocaust, approximately 230,000 people lost their lives during the 2004 earthquake/tsunami in Southeast Asia, and nearly 3,000 people died on 9/11. Did so many souls really agree before birth to die under these circumstances?

This question came up often during my workshops and honestly, I wasn't sure how to answer it. My training and experience wanted me to say "yes," but the sheer numbers of souls affected made it seem unfathomable. Then a friend introduced me to an article in Robert Schwartz's blog about between-life planning that helped shed light on the question.

In "What Is the Purpose of Catastrophic Events?,"[2] Schwartz wrote:

"I've received more questions about the pre-birth planning of large-scale, "negative" events. Let's take as an example the tsunami that hit

---

2 https://yoursoulsplan.wordpress.com/2017/11/28/
what-is-the-purpose-of-catastrophic-events/?fbclid=I-
wAR0hMuTbfit_ESOBZsZKKAWgI6SdAwizH0b9ZEon-
QU8Pu4Z52NL40PGyKu4

Southeast Asia a few years ago. More than 100,000 people were killed. My understanding is that those souls hoped before they were born that the Earth would be at a certain vibration by a certain point in linear time. These souls agreed before birth that if it looked as though the Earth were not going to get there, they would give their lives in a large-scale, natural disaster because they knew that the result would be a worldwide outpouring of love and compassion that would raise the Earth's vibration to the desired frequency."

You may recall that this is exactly what happened. The governments of the world put aside their differences and cooperated to funnel aid to Southeast Asia. This outpouring of love and compassion raised the frequency of our planet to the level those souls had intended.

You've probably heard the expression, "Where you stand depends upon where you sit." The tsunami is a great example of that expression. If you are a human who "sits" in the third dimension, then where you likely "stand" on the tsunami is that it was a terrible tragedy. If, however, you are a spirit guide who "sits" in the fourth dimension, then where you likely "stand" on the tsunami is that it was a great blessing to our world. Two diametrically opposed viewpoints, both of which are correct from the perspective of the observer.

As you look at the challenges in your own life, see if you can shift from the perspective of the personality to that of your soul. You will see your life in an entirely new light.

A Final Note on "Easy Lives"

"Why do some people seem to have it so easy in life?" This question was asked of me by a client who was still struggling with the sudden loss of her husband two years earlier. I have two answers for this question:

First, we never know what goes on behind closed doors. Some people work hard to keep their challenges private or hidden for reasons only they can answer. As a result, some people's lives appear easy when in fact they hide their struggles well.

Second, it does happen on occasion that a soul gets a lifetime of *rest* because several of the prior lifetimes were very challenging. In this example, the soul may be experiencing a life of financial comforts, full of love, and limited challenges.

I suggest we refrain from judging others for not having to deal with challenges because none of us ever really know all the details of another soul's lives.

What Lesson Did You Choose for This Life?

If you are curious as to what lesson you are working on in this lifetime, consider the recurrent themes that have been showing up in your life. These themes will provide you with clues and guide you to the likely lesson you chose to work on this time. For example, do you find yourself attracting the same negative personalities to your world? Do you continue to find yourself in the same dead-end jobs that do not excite you? If you look at your life from the perspective of learning, what do you think all of these characters and situations are trying to teach you? The following exercises will help you work through this question.

Exercises

The intention of this exercise is for you to con-template the challenges you have encountered in your life and what you learned as a result.

1. What is a recurrent challenge you have had in your life? Do you keep attracting the same wrong partners or friends? Do you keep letting others take advantage of you? Do you have difficulty keeping relationships? Do you continue to have health issues?

2. Choose one major challenge and write down how this challenge has continued to show up in your life.

3. Now I want you to identify what this continued challenge might be trying to teach you. Here are some examples: standing up for yourself, making your voice heard, taking care of your body, forgiveness, compassion for others, and so on. To do this part of the exercise, I recommend you make some quiet time for yourself. Sit for ten minutes and concentrate on slow, deep breaths to help yourself get to a light, meditative

state. Once you feel relaxed, ask yourself (out loud or silently), "What is my life challenge trying to teach me?" You might get the answer right away or it may take some time for the answer to become clear. The answer may come forward as a voice in your mind, a sense of knowing, or even your own voice telling you. Try your best to keep your ego mind out of the way.

CHAPTER 13

Between Life Regression

Though it is not my intention to go into detail about between life regressions in this beginner's guide, I do feel it will be beneficial to briefly describe the purpose and components of a typical session. Another common term for this type of regression is "life between lives." While the main purpose of a past life regression is to visit a past life that is affecting your life today, the main goal of a between life regression is to delve deeper into three components of your soul.

For a past life regression I use a light level of hypnosis to facilitate the session, also known as the alpha brain wave state. For a between life session to successfully take place, I help my clients go into a deeper hypnotized state known as the theta brain wave state, as described in Chapter 6. A between life regression lasts three to four hours and this deeper level of hypnosis accomplishes two things:

- ✿ Keeps the person in a relaxed state for the duration

- ✿ Facilitates working at a higher frequency for the entire session

A typical between-life session allows my client to visit a past life, meet with their high council, and visit the members of their soul group. A further description of the three components follows:

Past life—Similar to a past life regression, we visit a past life that is affecting my client's current life. After some work in this portion of the session with my client and their soul guide, I use this place to ask my client's guide if they have intentions for the remainder of the session or if we can make suggestions. Most often the guide will acquiesce to suggestions, at which point I state we would like to meet with the high council and soul group of my client. The soul guide typically guides my client to the next step, either the high council or the soul group.

High council—The council is comprised of benevolent entities who gather to answer questions and guide my client.

Although our soul guides have completed all of their Earthly incarnations and use their experiences to guide us, the high council members typically have not incarnated on Earth. The entities who make up the council reside at a very high frequency, hence the name "high council." The name does not infer that they are high and mighty beings overseeing us lowly Earth dwellers in our dense third dimension. They love us and truly want us to succeed in our soul evolution.

It is with the high council where I ask important questions on my client's behalf that have been prepared prior to the session. Beforehand, I ask my client to write a list of five to ten questions, in priority sequence (in case we don't have time to address all of them), comprised of what they want to ask their council regarding their life and soul. The most common questions are:

✿ What lesson did my client's soul choose to work on in their current incarnation?

✿ How is my client doing with that particular lesson? If the high council says my client isn't doing well, then I ask what my client may specifically do to get back on track.

✿ What was the purpose of my client getting cancer (or whatever physical or mental ailment they have or had) in their life?

✿ My client feels lost on his/her current career path. What can s/he do to find the right path?

✿ Is my client's soul an Earth soul or an Interplanetary soul? If the answer is Interplanetary, then I ask follow-up questions such as: Where did her soul come from? Can you show my client a scene from their soul's home place? What gift did my client's soul bring to Earth to share?

✿ My client has a challenging relationship with their mother/father/spouse in this lifetime. What can my client do in their current life to move forward with more peace and ease with that relationship?

⟪⟫

Soul group—When my client's guide takes them to visit their soul group, it's a very loving reunion. These souls typically greet the person with hugs and welcome the opportunity to visit with my client in this high-frequency realm.

As mentioned in Chapter 9 about soul groups, my client is meeting with the higher selves of the incarnated soul group members; therefore, they are very loving and accepting, regardless of the interpersonal issues they may be having with one another in their physical incarnations.

The pertinent soul group members who come forward to visit with my client will often answer questions that my client prepared before the session. For example, if my client has/had a challenging relationship with their mother, then I will ask questions of their mother's soul as to the source of the strain in the relationship.

Sometimes the challenge might be an issue the mother's soul has or had to work on in her current lifetime; other times it's a challenge the two souls have been working on for multiple lifetimes. I will also ask the various souls what my client can do to help work through any relationship issues in their current life.

I have included a few books in the Recommended Readings section of the Appendix that further explain between-life and life-between-lives regressions. It's a fascinating topic and one I encourage you to read more about if this book piqued your interest.

CHAPTER 14

Lasting Thoughts

As I conclude this beginner's guide to past life regression work, I want to leave you with some lasting thoughts as you contemplate all that you have read.

First of all, it has been a dream of mine to share this content with you in book form that I have been communicating orally for years in client sessions, workshops, and speaking engagements. What you do from this point on is your free will whether you pursue the topic further or set it aside thinking "that was interesting" or disregarding it completely. I respect all choices.

Second, please know that you are never alone in this life. Whether you are in your darkest moments or your brightest days, surrounded by family and friends or alone, your soul guide is always with you. Your guide is loving, compassionate, and never judges you. If you have never felt the presence of your guide and would like to do so, remember to get to a quiet place and ask your guide to help you connect. It takes practice, meditation, and possibly some casual walks in nature to connect with your guide but it can be done.

Third, the most common response I receive from my clients' guides when I ask, "What advice can you provide my client as they move forward in this life?" is, "Don't take life so seriously, have some fun!" Because our life challenges can easily consume us, it's important to make time for fun, laughter, and pursuing our interests and passions.

It has been a pleasure for me to share what I have learned so far.

Thank You,
Shelly

Glossary of Terms

Current life—The life you are living today. You have a birth date but no death, passing, or transition date yet.

Earth souls—All incarnations of these souls have occurred on Earth.

Empath—An individual who is highly sensitive to the mental and physical energy around them, especially the energy of other people. Some empaths have difficulty protecting their senses from the negative energy of others and sometimes internalize this energy.

Frequency–Spiritual frequency can be defined as the rate at which we vibrate spiritually. It is the rate at which our spiritual energy vibrates. The feeling of love is a high frequency, whereas the feeling of hate is a low frequency. Deceased loved ones, soul guides, high council members, and guardian angels reside in a realm considered to be at a high frequency.

Future life—A lifetime that has not yet begun. For a soul, this life is planned to occur sometime in the future.

High council—A group of benevolent beings who love and guide our soul throughout its evolution. They are called "high council" due to the high frequency at which these entities reside.

Higher self—The portion of your soul that remains in the soul realm when you are incarnated on Earth. Our physical bodies on Earth cannot contain 100 percent of our soul, as it's too much energy. Our higher self also acts as our guide during our Earth incarnations.

Interplanetary soul—An evolved soul from another planet, star, or galaxy, who has spent most of its incarnations somewhere other than Earth. These souls come to Earth to share their spiritual gifts to help humanity evolve.

Karma—Refers to the spiritual principle of cause and effect, wherein intent and actions of an individual influence the future of that individual.

Past life—A prior life that has ended. A soul's past life will have a birth date and a death date. Past lives are visited by people to provide insight into aspects of their current lives.

Reiki—A healing technique based on the therapist channeling energy into a patient via their hands. This process activates the natural healing processes of the patient's body and can restore physical and emotional well-being.

Soul guide—An advanced, benevolent soul who resides in the soul realm and guides you during and between your earthly incarnations. Same as a spirit guide; term is used interchangeably.

Soul memory—The complete memory of all your lifetimes and experiences in between lifetimes that is stored with your soul.

Soul realm—The place I refer to in this book where a soul resides when it's not incarnate in human form. There are many dimensions to the soul realm and this can be referred to as heaven by some. For use in this book, the soul realm is where soul guides, soul groups, and high councils meet with my clients during a regression session.

Spirit guide—Same as soul guide; terms are often used interchangeably.

Third dimension—The Earth realm.

Transition—A common term in spiritual books and language to mean the passing or death of a person. Example: "He transitioned this morning from cancer."

Vibration—Spiritual vibrations are *pure spirit energy*—the stuff of which consciousness is made. Energy has no mass and no properties itself. In order for energy to make a difference in the world—and for all intents and purposes, to exist—it must vibrate. Every action and every thought creates vibrations in the spiritual energy field.

Recommended Readings

The Classics

These are books written before the year 2000 by people I consider to be pioneers of contemporary past-life regression therapy.

Many Lives, Many Masters,
by Brian L. Weiss, MD

Journey of Souls: Case Studies of Life Between Lives,
by Michael Newton, PhD

Letters from the Afterlife: A Guide to the Other Side,
by Elsa Barker

Reincarnation and Karma,
by Edgar Cayce, Scott R. Pollak, et al.

Contemporary Works

This is a shortlist of the many books written about past life and between life regression. I have also listed many works that have been influential toward my learning as well as books I have referenced in this book.

Bringing Your Soul to Light: Healing through Past Lives and the Time Between,
by Dr. Linda Backman

The Evolving Soul: Spiritual Healing through Past Life Exploration,
by Dr. Linda Backman

Souls on Earth: Exploring Interplanetary Past Lives,
by Dr. Linda Backman

Your Soul's Plan: Discovering the Real Meaning of the Life You Planned Before You Were Born,
by Robert Schwartz

Your Soul's Gift: The Healing Power of the Life You Planned Before You Were Born,
by Robert Schwartz

The Afterlife of Billy Fingers: How My Bad-Boy Brother Proved to Me There's Life After Death,
by Annie Kagan

Leap of Faith: Transforming Physical and Emotional Pain into Spiritual Growth,
by Jeffrey D. Millman, MD

Dying to Be Me: My Journey from Cancer to Near Death to True Healing,
by Anita Moorjani

Many recent books
by Dr. Brian Weiss

E-Squared: Nine Do-It-Yourself Energy Experiments That Prove Your Thoughts Create Your Reality,
by Pam Grout

Books for interplanetary souls

Souls on Earth: Exploring Interplanetary Past Lives,
by Dr. Linda Backman

Keepers of the Garden,
by Dolores Cannon

Books for empaths

The Children of Now: Crystalline Children, Indigo Children, Star Kids, Angels on Earth, and the Phenomenon of Transitional Children,
by Meg Blackburn Losey, PhD

The Indigo Children: The New Kids Have Arrived,
by Lee Carroll and Jan Tober

The Empath's Survival Guide: Life Strategies for Sensitive People,
by Judith Orloff, MD

Suicide Prevention Resources

National Suicide Prevention Lifeline, 1-800-273-8255
Emergency number 911
www.cdc.gov/suicide/

Training Providers for Past-Life and Between-Life Regression Therapists

Dr. Linda Backman's school, established in 1997,

The Raven Heart Center, located in Boulder, Colorado. www.ravenheartcenter.com*

Dr. Brian Weiss's school. www.brianweiss.com

Dolores Cannon and her school's Quantum Healing Hypnosis Technique. www.QHHTofficial.com
*I was trained at Dr. Backman's school.

ABOUT THE AUTHOR

SHELLY PIERSON is committed to facilitating the process in which an individual may recognize the patterns embedded in one's current life so as to appreciate and come to know their own soul and thereby improve their lives. The death of a brother and a lecture by Dr. Jeffrey D. Millman stimulated her to read every book she could find and attend various seminars on past life experiences. She followed her interest into formal training in past-life and between-life regression therapy, which then became her new career. Using her new credentials and knowledge, she began facilitating regressions for individuals and leading workshops to familiarize people from all walks of life about the idea that our soul memory carries all knowledge of past life experiences that impact our present lives. This book is a composite of her experience in introducing concepts of reincarnation and soul memory of past lives as well as work with guides and mentors between lives on a broader scale and to assist people in learning about the beauty, the true depth of their souls.

In addition to a B.S. in computer information systems, an MBA, and certification in project management, Shelly is also a certified past life and between-life regression therapist, having been trained by Dr. Linda Backman of the Raven Heart Center in Colorado. Shelly divides her time between Reno, Nevada and the Big Island of Hawaii.

For more information, visit Shelly's website:
www.N2Souls.com